"Littlevoice"

Missing Peace

Reflect!

Think!

Poetry!

Cherish!

Debate!

Love...

Change!

Smile!

Happiness!

Missing Peace

"Littlevoice"

Author H. K. Stokes

Published by Dolman Scott Ltd

Copyright 2013 © H. K. Stokes text

Copyright 2013 © Dreamstime stock photography

Dreamstime can be found www.dreamstime.com

First printed in Great Britain in 2013 by Dolman Scott

ISBN 978-1-909204-21-8

Dolman Scott

www.dolmanscott.com

Dedicated to Valerie Stokes

This book is dedicated to Valerie Stokes. Val passed away on the 30th August 2008 age 62. She fought breast cancer for 18 years, during which time she obtained a Diploma in Management studies at South Bank University for her job, which was Training Centre Manager for Kent Fire and Rescue Service.

Val learned to live each day to the full; a brave and courageous person. Her great love our two girls Andrea and Kayla, she felt blessed that she witnessed the birth of her three grandchildren Beth, Molly, and Ella Hope. She had an input to the name Ella Hope.

Val wrote poetry for family and friends mainly comedic rhyming verse for special occasions. Her last poem ironically was for her own 60th Birthday called Val's Sixtieth, which I have started this book with. Val was the inspiration for me to start writing poetry, I am sure she would be pleased and happy that I have taken up the mantle she left behind.

Valerie recited her work to camera on the balcony of The Cavalletto Hotel in Venice whilst on our last holiday, which I now treasure on a DVD.

Acknowledgements

I have recently been lucky enough to meet Richard W Jenkins. We both write on writers-network.com. He has taught poetry for some forty-five years, and kindly has agreed to tutor me. I have only had a few weeks instruction and already notice a vast difference in my approach. I am taking a gap to finish the groundwork for this book before going back with him.

Also would like to thank a lifetime friend Alan Ross for helping me to put together the manuscript for this project, page numbering, sizing and pulling together as one file for printing. A much deeper thank you for all the support he has given me over these past few years which have been difficult times.

Lastly to Valerie Leach, a big thank you for your woodland water colour that steered me down a particular path and so the poem "He Waits" was born and became an acrylic print with her fine water colour as the backdrop.

Preface

My poetry was born from an immense love of a pure soul mate, a best friend and, proudly, my wife. The grief of losing her, to cancer, left a crazed mind searching to find something or someone that could possibly take her place. Sorry, the answer is NO WAY! Perhaps I need to look for someone very different. However, I have found POETRY that has been cathartic and a help to console my grief.

It all began with me looking for something unique for Val's birthday. She had written poems for friends and family on special occasions so I thought, "why not write one dedicated to her". It took in excess of a month to write and the poem is called 'Valerie My Love'. It portrays our life together from the day we met. She was 21 years old. I proposed on our first date, she accepted. We waited for two years to save enough money to pay for a deposit on a house. We were together for forty-two years and married for thirty-nine of those years. I seriously cannot remember once during that time raising our voices in a row. I am not saying we didn't have some ups and downs, just that I was extremely lucky; some would say we both were.

If I had the ability to grant wishes I would restrict myself to just one. You could come to me with the wish that your relationship lasts as long and is as fulfilling as ours was. I would grant that wish for anyone and everyone because, I believe, we should all be blessed with the chance to experience our life with a true soul mate.

Now the pain: when we reach the moment that special person is taken from us, a period that I would not wish on my worst enemy. However hard as it is to accept at the time, I am glad that the saying is true: time does help to heal. Albeit, you have a richness of memories never to be forgotten, that will be with you until it's your turn to depart. I am not a religious man but I do hope to meet Val again in some experience of an afterlife.

My poetry has developed from its natural rawness and I have begun to spread my wings and started to write and comment on a range of themes from grief to love, to some social comment and to the futility of war. It is my hope that some of these poems strike a chord that, as a reader, you will find helpful and either agree or disagree with; but the poems will, at the very least, ignite a spark that interests you enough to discuss with friends, colleagues and family.

All I ask is for you to ENJOY!

Ken Stokes (Littlevoice)

Forward

Ken was born on May 1st 1944 in Stoke Newington, London. The family moved to White City when he was five years old. He grew up in this area of West London and attended Canberra Primary School and then progressed on to Christopher Wren School. His secondary schooling was an unhappy time as he was streamed into an engineering curriculum (due to parental influence) rather than an arts based curriculum that had been recommended by the school.

At sixteen Ken became an apprentice Fitter-Machinist with London Transport but could not wait to complete the apprenticeship, finally being released at the age of twenty-two. For a couple of years he had great fun driving for a small company belonging to a friend's father. The company hired out specialised vehicles to film and television units. Ken worked on films such as "The Dirty Dozen", "Salt and Pepper" and many other well-known productions.

Ken met Valerie when he was 23 years old and he knew that his future would be with her. However, his plans for their life together required a change of direction to enable his earnings to match impending needs such as a wedding and a house. So Ken embarked on a career in sales and marketing.

Valerie and Ken were married in the summer of 1969; Ken 25 and Valerie 23 years old and they moved to a new semi in Caversham Park Village near Reading, and commenced their blissful life together. Two beautiful daughters, Andrea and Kayla, resulted from their loving relationship. A move for the family to Lordswood, in Kent, was made possible when Ken was promoted to a Sales Manager. Ken still resides at this address today, albeit, now on his own, and has retired after a long and rewarding career.

Poetry was initially Valerie's domain with Ken being asked, from time to time, to contribute sundry inspiration. When Valerie was taken from him he immersed himself in writing his own poetry and found this to be an emotional and liberating journey away from his enormous grief. His first poem "Valerie my Love" was the catalyst for many more that form the basis of this poetry volume.

His poems are, in fact, his thoughts in rhyme with, of course, some artistic licence. He encompasses a broad spectrum of subjects that add interest to the content of the book. You, the reader, can agree or disagree with his views; his hope is that the poems inspire debate and, hopefully, some will bring a smile. Ken hopes that you enjoy this book.

Contents

Chapter one

Love Poems

Chapter two

Grief Poems

Chapter Three

Nature Poems

Chapter Four

Heston Blumenthal

Chapter Five

Protest Poems

Chapter Six

Social Comment
      Poems

Chapter Seven

Comedy Poems

Chapter Eight

Family and Friends
Poems

Val's Sixtieth

The time has come and now it's here.
It comes around each time, each year.
But this time, Shall I be shifty,
Or own up to being — Ooh Sixty!

Have been with Ken since '69'.
Our time together has been just fine.
Throughout that time had ups and downs.
Which sometimes caused a lot of frowns.

Into our life two daughters came.
Bringing them up - oh what a game.
A sense of humour, you did need.
To do it properly and give a lead.

They're grown up now, different girls they are.
One has made me a proud grandma.
The other one has itchy feet;
to have her home becomes a treat.

Two Granddaughters to keep me fit.
I love it when I can do my bit.
It's really good when I can phone,
and say, it's time to take them home.

My size 10 figure, where has it gone?
Over the years, it's gone on and on.
I used to wear a small bikini!
Reduced now, a large tankini!

My natural brown hair, its gone too.
From a bottle now, will have to do.
Never mind what will be will be.

I maybe sixty but at least;
I still have my own teeth.
The memory it's true I struggle.
I always get into a muddle.

My family, new friends and old.
Need I think to be told.
How much they all mean to me.
They keep me strong, I'm sure you see.

Over the years we've shed some tears.
We've also had a lot of fears.
But blessed am I, I do believe.
Be Positive, you can achieve.

Throughout the years my rock is Ken,
ever constant now and then.
Like a roof both sides needs support;
my girls, I know I'm in their thought.

Another stage in life I start.
Determined that I will not part;
from loved one's, friends and all.
I still intend to have — a ball!

Valerie Stokes
@2006

Chapter One

Love Poems

Poems of love and romance, the author calls upon personal situations for inspiration. He then uses poetic licence in the way one would sprinkle fields with dancing red poppies, a sight to catch your breath. A mood to carry you on an enchanting journey.

Valerie my Love

A chance meeting in King Street Hammersmith our lives it did define.
Glancing into your eyes a mirror to our future — yours and mine.
To say that I knew, may be slightly bold, a vision I would say!
"Yes" to a date, meant my life was complete forever and a day.
Forty-two years, living as one, sharing, caring, winter and sun.
A family two daughters to raise, times we had, memories, the fun!

The thunderbolt delivered, "Cancer" he said.
The strength and the courage, the tears that we shed.
For some eighteen years, through the ups and the downs.
We had good times, few bad times, times when we'd frown.
Fight all gone, no fight left, time to close your eyes.
Relax let be... shed tears, loved ones — hear our cries.

The fire service your chosen career second family became.
Commitment never in question, qualifications in a frame.
Tireless hours working, degree required, even in burden achieved!
A win-win partnership for you both, a role you would never leave.
You both respect and are respected, proof shown as we faced the end.
My sense of pride at your accomplishments, for you my wife, my friend.

Main passion travel, a large part in your life.
A porter with your luggage, glad you're my wife.
Such valued memories, might have never been.
The many places I might have never seen.
Last trip Venice; your sixtieth... celebrate.
A travel finale — yes it was, just great!

Survival comes making an active day with more and more to do.
The house it is now complete, room by room, without you to approve.
The garden next, 'twas our sanctuary, the place we both enjoyed.
Once complete, your memory be centre stage, no one to remove.
Torn between the crematorium or here, where I want to be.
With visions of an even better place, somewhere for you and me.

Valerie, my love, here in my mind, so real.
Your scent, your voice, your touch via my DVD's remind.
Each morning awake — determine how I feel.
A good or bad day for me, myself to find.
Just another sad day, one more day to grind.
Alone with you my love, just you on my mind.

As yet another day it closes, to an end when darkness comes.
Once more to bed I clamber enforced, to slip unconsciously numb.
Projects with jobs galore, much difficulty when visiting old chums.
Is this forever my life without you? The whole thing seems surreal.
My sense of life has now gone, just leaving confusion in its wake.
Perhaps, one day some meaning may return, my life again to make.

To live my life again some things I wouldn't change.
One, I'm sure, King Street Hammersmith I'd arrange.
Wisdom's shown, life's full of good, bad, cruel and kind.
Soul mates should be there for everyone to find.
Hell's on earth our daughter says, some to be freed.
If true, knowledge gained, you've reached your destiny.

If heaven exists you're there, my angel sent to love and care.
A film I watched said a bell must ring for angels to gain their wings.
Now our wedding video, St Martins with more than one bell rings.
Your wings now yours with more to give away, see you in our garden.
Each... every day. Unconditional love means wings will be abound.
Each pair a special gift from your hands, old and new friends will be found.

I know at rest so many for you to find.
With a bright white light to guide from inside... kind.
The shell that bound, tied you to this earth now gone.
That inner light, your eyes and smile that just shone.
In memory whilst on this soil I must tread.
You'll live on in thoughts that are inside my head.

Just one last request, not deserved it's true, please save one pair of wings.
I know someone not far — anything would do to fly again with you.
Forever, it's endless left missing someone in truth — emptiness.
Difficult you see, think our lives will cross once more brings hope to me.
Together once again how near, how far I feel subsiding pain.
Surface it's true, underneath, deep the actor rears his head again.

I Luv You

Ken

Sealed With A Kiss

Expectation of a nation, watched on by the world.
Ceremony and tradition, with our emotions, they've twirled.
Our Royal family for us, from British stock that's the best.
We watch on surely knowing, this union it is blessed.
Lightly stepped onto our streets from the Goring Hotel,
a deep breath inhaled by all, "God speed we wish you well!"
The dress some say inspired by Princess Grace of Monaco
our nation do we mind, let out that breath and swallow.
William arrives escorted by Harry his best man,
both uniforms look dapper, try to beat that if you can.
Slight hesitation etched on his brow, while brother grins,
Now's the time to set aside, releasing all those sins.
Your Bride is on her way, to the roaring of the crowd,
hear it from the alter of the Abbey it's so loud.
Gliding serenely hand on father's gosh, he is proud.
Harry's glance, he makes his comment, from us all to shroud.
Stood by his side, he looks... beauty he confirms to all.
He knows throughout these years, reasons why he had to fall.
Who gives this woman to this man, her hand passed with pride,
all men who have given daughters, tears are hard to hide.
The archbishop pronounces, they are now man and wife.
Near two billion people wishing both the best for life.
How strange is this feeling, crosses boundaries and class,
his eyes clear to see... a pedestal he stands his lass.
Stepping out into the sun, for the world to adore.
Open coach to the palace, tantalising rapport.
The crowds going wild just to catch a glimpse of them both.
Royal couple in Westminster Abbey given their troth.
The stage set, the final scene of scenes, crowds all in bliss.
Famous palace balcony, where they seal it with a kiss.
No disappointment, one more ~ lip readers see him say.
They drive into the sunset; today's been a good day.

Angel Of The North

Angels are rarely seen on earth, somehow we know they care.
Comforting when travelling north to see her standing there.
With majesty, she surveys from height, imposing... her size.
Somehow you float seem to fly just to look into her eye's.

Travellers who pass this site, Gateshead the arterial A1.
Hope and pray for a warm summer day, backdrop in the sun.
She welcomes all who travel north, to keep from any harm.
Serenely guides all those who pass, with her commanding charm.

Adventure starts, for it is a mere mortal angel that I seek
Travelling north along this road, thoughts of her I am weak
This solid image seems to point the way – a future bright.
Shows journeys are not all by road, for some you need to fight.

For those of us more fortunate, we are blessed we find love.
Another soul, warm and sensual slips into like a glove.
Now this angel who's welcome as I pass, is guiding me.
Showing that my first true love is now time, to set her free.

The journey home I visited a pilgrimage, rebirth.
Finding someone who's bringing joy, and yes she's here on earth.
Perhaps now I have three angels, my future have in mind;
who willingly have helped me, for a love once more to find.

Light of heart and light of step, is what love just does for you.
It's Happiness you must snatch when found, as you're passing through.
This awe-inspiring statue, beneath its frame, beats a heart,
and joined together two as one, live again – life restart.

Love's Disguise

Love strikes in many a disguise,
felt mostly with a heart beat rise.

Other signs I am sure you'll know,
that tingling feeling, head to toe.

It can be a strength that attracts,
of love, we know numerous facts.

Yes strike it does without a thought,
now in it's web, you can be caught.

Perhaps creep up just like a cat,
once we know, we just doff our hat.

It's linked with a heady perfume;
for others, now there is no room.

Gently sinking deep into bliss,
vision those soft lips, that soft kiss.

Both entwined in this ancient game,
love not lust, they are not the same.

Once confident we know, we know,
to the ends of the earth we'll go.

Yes give up all that we can see,
to spend a life, just you and me.

He Waits

He sits, he waits on grassy slopes,
a true love for to spy.
Eyes cast across the fields in hope,
another day ~ a sigh.

Through woodland mists a vision's formed;
imagery clear in mind.
Seeing her skip from tree to tree;
he knows she is his kind.

His heart knows pain from love before;
a love that has been lost.
For now he seeks a second love;
Fearful... what this will cost?

Living our lives, each in surprise,
the roads we choose are new.
Submerged in memories from ... past;
our time, thus far, just flew.

When gold's been struck and life's been lived,
unknowingly ... fulfilled,
the inner greed for more is deep;
his cup half full, not spilled.

Now, each breath we take is precious;
at least, once more we live.
Gifted with so much love inside,
strong feelings ~ more to give.

In this shell that he hath borrowed;
now, is a little worn.
This heart, so loud that beats inside;
still, strong as its day born.

He sits he waits on grassy slopes
a true love for to spy.
Eyes cast across the fields in hope,
another day ~ a sigh.

These treasures sought, the woods reveal;
before his new love — he will kneel.

7

Yonder Field

Hand in Hand ~ vision as they tread;
journey's end ... yonder field.
As hearts attune beat soft in-time,
their love to be revealed.

Young virgins meeting, yet untouched.
The cherry blossoms show;
beneath together yearn to lay,
our lovers' cheeks aglow.

The pace picks up, for both a smile;
shines moisture on each brow.
Breath quickens with each step they take,
a warmth in loins — allow.

Destination, the tree they touch;
spread blankets on the ground.
Both, in each other's arms they lay;
long waited, love's been found.

Eyes blinking twice as light strikes brain,
she sleeps – to wake again.

Bat Squeak

Out of the blackness of sleep; abyss of despair.
Visions of her floating, reveals you truly care.
Relentlessly, time passes; to terms you must come.
Taking, a close look at life, and join in its hum.

It's grief that consumes us when a loved one departs.
Now destroyed, it's pain and anguish, our broken hearts.
Feel like an amputee, learning to walk once more.
Take one step at a time, as I cover the floor.

Come to terms, this tragedy that life has imposed;
never to forget, but this chapter is now closed.
You'll take from this experience all that is good.
A key to open new doors, it's time now you should.

Life having much that sparkles and much that is great.
To miss out on what's offered, surely not too late.
Gently, as you close the lid on what's now your past,
allow your eyes ... open to see again at last.

Light slowly increasing a mirror and a smile;
look carefully, the image just stare for a while.
Let go, farewell, au revoir, see you again.
Time to lift your heart – time to remove all this pain.

You must open the door now, let in this new light,
like a blind man very slowly – regaining sight.
The things are on offer, when you let people in.
Open up your heart, to let a new life begin.

Never, find the Holy Grail, that tiny "Bat Squeak."
Indicates love, legs start to wobble knees go weak.
This state of confusion able to hear your heart,
The pace that it's thumping at, perhaps not so smart.

All your experience just sit back take care – think.
Companionship, laughter, soul mate, nod and a wink.
With all now on offer, make the circle complete.
A new partner, friend, lover, whom I wish to meet.

I see you

See you with my eyes,
touch with my body.
My lips will explore.
My tongue to excite.
My heart is to love.
In mind day and night.
Our journey unmapped.
As we two take flight,
new life to begin.
Both reaching new heights,
completely loved up.
Race nor black or white,
inner self we see.
Hand in hand to walk,
together will be.

I see you,
You see me.

As Love Grows

Vision can attract or repel,
just a touch or even a smell.
Layers for us, that will reveal,
once exposed we hope, will appeal.

When we know time is on our side,
inner secrets, we will confide.
Hope the majority you'll accept,
some I don't mind, if you reject.

Like a seed from soil that will grow,
a seed we're both happy to sow.
Togetherness means compromise,
of this there can be no disguise.

A willingness yes we will learn,
respect and love we both will earn.
Some things are there for us to see,
true love's not purchased, it is free.

It is said, "what will be will be."
Where will it go we now will see?
Let's both ensure that we have fun,
an inner warmth, an inner sun.

As love grows, it bubbles within.
Time now... begin a new begin.
This happiness so rarely seen,
memories from once when a teen.

A Virginal Child

As we embark a new journey of love,
with thoughts sent, from heaven above.
We have the mind of a virginal child,
all our senses primed running wild.

Excitement is coursing through every vain,
blank... memories... previous pain.
Along this tightrope we carefully tread.
Ignoring views, others have said.

The stakes always seem set so very high;
reach out, feel you can touch the sky.
Once you're there, it is such a long way back.
Your eyes blinded to any crack.

That first twinge as it exposes each nerve.
Teeth crunching ice that's being served.
The chill, as it tingles, runs down your spine.
In your heart hope — all will be fine.

You think it's your head in control of this scene,
you doubt her love — is she your queen?
You muster all your strength; it's time to fight,
open your eyes, no sleep tonight.

Once more drowning in this dark lonely place,
mirror not reflecting your face.
For some of us, it's just not meant to be.
Thoughts turning dark, setting one free.

Now is the time to reflect once again.
Life, it can bring us so much pain.
If meant to be, surely left up to fate.
Touch love once more seemingly great.

It is clear the first cut creates most pain.
When love beckons — will we feel it again?

My Heart

Gently placed my heart in your hand,
for you to draw ~ yours in the sand.

When you're ready if you would kneel,
bury mine below ~ show how you feel.

Two hearts as one, not to deny,
leaving both with wings, now can fly.

Together, a rich life to live,
with what is left, each other give.

Passion and laughter mixed with love,
ordained, from somewhere up above.

So hard for some — to be alone,
much more for those, who love have known.

They say there are soul mates to find,
if you look hard and stretch your mind.

Life is a gamble, take that chance;
with open heart, accept that dance.

Cupped softly in his hands lips kissed.
The glories of the things you've missed.

Little time left ... so much to see,
be so nice, if it were with me.

Flight

Flying in our dreams surly life's biggest treat,
with wings on our shoulders and wings on both feet.
Soaring through blue skies, heading up through a cloud,
excitement and ecstasy, scream out aloud!
They say we're at our best, when we've entered REM,
if in sleep you have flown, you want to again.
Closing eyes relax, sleep an incoming tide,
falling deeper, unconscious bliss, now can hide.
Flight in thought, is it fantasy, is it real?
Taking off, soar high in the sky, now to feel.
Touches your soul, adrenaline rush, feels right;
you now know this feeling, this thing they call flight.
Looping the loop, make your way back down to earth.
Memories committed, a smile that says mirth.
Delicately touch down, both feet on the ground.
Knowing you've landed with body and mind sound.
Experience all feelings, bodies entwined;
other heights to savour, I think you will find.
When two beings merge, to really become one;
puts a smile on your face, the warmth of the sun.
This journey begins, unexplored roads, to seek.
Hours and days pass us by, a year is a week.
Time like sand slips through our fingers and is gone.
Surely days precious, like a flashlight is shone;
switch on, and switch off in the blink of one's eye.
When something's real, worth having, don't say goodbye.
Move forward, touch finger tips, steel that first kiss.
You've entered a state, that's referred to as bliss.
Savour, relish new feelings that come your way.
Set minds to autopilot, your flight's today.

A Good Life

I awake with the light, striking my brain.
A small yawn and a stretch, another day.
Lay wondering, un-planned events to come;
yet underpinned, with things that I must do.
Cautiously, legs emerge from the duvet,
both feet touching the warmth of the carpet.
With a firm push on the mattress – vertical
Catching my reflection in the mirrored door,
a smile touches my lips as she is here.
She **was**, she **is** ~ **forever** she will **be**.
This my reason why it's a good life for me.

Always Faithful

Rosie is my name,
rosy is my nature.
I am just grateful,
always be faithful.

I awake each day,
my head's saying play.
My mum takes the lead,
then find myself freed.

The grass feels so good,
as I pound the ground.
Stretching each sinew,
my ears cocked for sound

A whistle a shout,
a quick turnabout.
To your side I run,
"Oh" I have such fun.

Return home blissful,
never less faithful.
Naturally so loyal,
around your feet coil.

Softly I will sleep,
with one eye, I peep.
For you to keep safe,
I'm always faithful.

Summer Love

On my quest to find a soul mate,
are miles important, or just fate.

Journeys made surely will be fine,
look with care we'll both see a sign.

Like a mirror our eyes reflect;
both knowingly not — to expect.

Nurture this summer love to grow.
A special seed, we both must sow.

Scarborough to meet by the sea.
A vision ~ my heart you've set free.

We stroll, we talk, we're hand in hand.
My heart is pounding feel so grand.

Back home with both feet on the ground;
could this be love, that we have found.

Our lips they touched for me the key,
over time, what will be — will be.

Recaptured youth, and times gone by;
you bring a smile ~ you bring a sigh.

Chosen you

My sweet heart, I have chosen you.
Reflect, you've chosen me.
Favouring each other, our life;
for us, will always be.

The bride-to-be prepares and preens.
Perfection through his eyes.
Seeing her glide across the floor;
this, one of life's great highs.

Stunning so beautiful, eyes freeze.
A vision from the Gods.
Perfect angel ~ who sits before,
now is mine, at any odds.

My turn to now impress my bride.
I promise I'll work hard.
I scrub up well I hope she'll see,
no wish, to leave her scarred.

The day it came and began well.
As friends start to arrive.
We both can hear our hearts beating.
Linked on a high — alive.

Travel in our chariot of love.
To the chapel we'll wed.
Friends and family gather around
to watch us breaking bread.

The day seems like a vision... dream.
All there—yet only one;
for me, a realm above the rest.
She is my moon, my sun.

All too quickly this day it ends;
as day turns into night.
Good memories with thoughts flood back.
None more than my first sight.

As days go "The best" comes to mind.
Somehow know, many more we'll find.

That Touch

Reflecting in her eyes, scene's so sad.
A life behind lived full.
An inner strength that needs support.
A softness touching wool.

Left to cope still remaining strong.
Heart aching for that touch.
A soul that is in need of glue.
A shoulder or a crutch.

Matriarch please do not abuse.
Unconditional love.
Her family will always sit first.
A comforting white dove.

A woman whose passions show.
In her every sweet smile.
A choice for him to wonder on.
Perhaps — linger a while.

Before you cause heartache and pain.
Think carefully my friend.
You have a woman, not a toy.
Be gentle in the end.

Exposing ourselves on the net,
seeking things that we've lost.
For two souls to completely bind.
Beware for those, the cost.

Each breath we take switches a light;
clearer for us to see.
A leap of faith perhaps to show,
this journey you and me.

Promises are known to be thin,
seems pain and love unite.
We're placing ourselves in danger,
Be sure it's worth the fight.

Final word is fun can be had,
if not forever don't be sad.

Love Land

Know love land's a beautiful place,
those reside there, just look at their face.
Eyes with a smile and tightness of skin.
Look at those lips just look at that grin.

Love land's magic a wonderful place.
Whoever we are we're in this race.
Heart pumping blood with vigour and pace.
Mystical hand moves to an embrace.

Age no barrier to fall to this fate.
All we need is to find the right mate.
Seems we are stuck, despite our best plan.
Lighting strikes randomly — if it can.

For those looking, just turn to the skies.
Mirror lightning reflects in your eyes.
Flash you've been struck there's no turning back.
You're caught... love land your heart an attack.

Should you desire to meet someone new,
when embarked on this road, follow through.
No doubt in my mind writing this line.
A move to love land all will be fine.

Most live in hope, get caught, feel this pain.
Once touched we need again and again.
Some say "It's only a state of mind."
Let me assure, it's love you will find.

From a Distance

From a distance my love, is this secret just for He.
Invisibly in the wings he waits for you to see.
Enigmatically glides into view — smile precedes.
Heart swelling pounds in his chest, his pulse begins to speed.
Shoulder length red hair flowing with a wisp and a curl.
Lose all sense this vision sends, his head into a whirl.
Petite, so delicate from inside she shows such strength;
knowing that these feelings, forever kept at arms length.
Tormented your search perfection you can almost touch.
Deep down aware the answer — just use it as a crutch.
Each visit confirms love, does she know that he is there.
A vision from enforced distance would she even care.
We walk this hallowed soil not knowing others' regard.
Perhaps lives to be enhanced, with compliments not barred.
Once she knows just how he feels it could be a surprise.
Willing thy reply, could be love shining in her eyes.
As we get older — losing the optimism of youth.
Hiding behind these closed curtains, not to know the truth.
Deep down the will is still there, passion it still bubbles.
Fear and embarrassment would get him into trouble.
Is it right these feelings, subdued, the words gone unsaid.
Chemistry disregarded from confrontation fled.
Could have been made in heaven for life a perfect match.
Thinking a last chance at love for happiness to snatch.
Seems senseless creating so much pain for you alone.
Now honour and dignity in your life you have shown.
Restrained from committing, exposing what might have been;
Imagination consummates, happiness your queen.
You have stepped back from the brink, perhaps a hornets' nest.
Thinking, for you to deal with your life, which has been blessed
Proudly, have chosen a road, keep other folk at bay.
By choosing the right path, others' happiness can stay.

Rock of Love

Therein lies beauty this rock found.
Nurtured by hands unknown.
Nature's pure engineering feat.
Not ugly — for men grown.

Eyes able to see beyond realm.
Vision can shape and plane.
Cuts and polishes till complete.
Beauty called — his refrain.

Adorn her body ~ one we love.
What's seen, sure now is worth.
Framed parts thus enhanced, they glitter
with gifts from "Mother Earth".

Who now is it has won her heart?
Her love or diamantaire?
His choice her inner mind has moved.
This master ~ is that fair?

Seems wherever man goes to breathe.
Search for air clean and free.
A new love there is to be sought.
Adorned with rocks to see.

A diamond saying keep at bay.
This hand's a hand for two.
A rock now binding this young love.
Is saying "I Love You".

The true wealth surfaced cannot hide.
For him the master her ~ the bride.

Our Child

Conceived from love conceived from joy.
As parents matters not, a girl, a boy.
Our hearts and minds, they're all in tact,
First cursory glance, confirming this fact.

Look down in wonder so strong, brave.
Living nine months in a watery cave.
Freedom nigh — signs the time is right.
Born into this world, just follow the light.

Arrived — this delicate bundle.
Wish the crying was more of a mumble.
Pleased you have all your bits in tact.
Our new father has this breeding thing cracked.

Time goes so quickly, passes by.
Blossoms growing her hands touching the sky.
Children born should fulfill their dream.
Wise parents knowing not all it would seem.

When dreams fulfilled, a sense of pride.
Winning or losing is the fun — don't hide.
Worlds full of much wonder to see.
To experience it — you need be free.

What makes us whole — learning to cope.
Each day lessons learned and absorbed I hope.
Most meaningful passed on, we give.
Learn to be humble with confidence live.

Our hope is you move forward go enjoy your life.
Meeting the right person become husband and wife.

Lay with Me

Come lay with me
Love with our eyes
Talk through silence
Yet say so much
Lips touch gently
Tasting passion
Nose rubbing nose
Finger tips press
Firmly run nails
Down outstretched arm
To meet her breast
Cupping squeezing
To meet with lips
Dancing dart tongue
Nipples sing ~ rise
An inner warmth
Between her thighs
The serpent flicks
Her love cup fill
Head in places,
to taste and thrill.
Her love to drink.
Eyes meeting eyes
Connection made
Two into one
Sense ~ ecstasy
Minds are floating
Body seizures
Tandem climax
Calling his name
Be still, relax
Lips meet again
Come lay with me

Fulfillment

Life moves in such mysterious ways,
warm flesh to see — over which to gaze.
Stomach ties itself into a knot.
Mind now drifting to places ... are hot.
Look into those eyes and you can see,
through windows to her soul, set her free;
Purpose, touching flesh ignites – mind games,
what's seen is sensual, frame by frame.
Heat playing with each and every sense,
a prepared warrior, sinews tense.
Flesh touches flesh a lightning flash.
The gift of oneself not bought with cash.
This passion chemistry has unleashed.
Love brims to the top on which to feast.
Worry not if lust or love my sweet,
for they are one once our bodies meet.
Waves of emotion, to raise the stake,
hand in glove connection — love to make.
Renewed vigour to feel the power,
five fingers gently tease, the flower.
Heat raised temperature running high,
to meet our maker, to touch the sky.
Quietly absorb, all around this scene,
two people touched as one, now have been.
The gift of gifts that has since been shared,
our inner soul to each is now bared.
Depth of peace, tranquillity to find,
fulfillment — both body and our mind.

Exposed to Love Again

Exposed to love, when it's been submerged for a while.
You find yourself deep in thought, on your lips a smile.
A honey bee skipping from — blossom to blossom.
Coursing through every vein, feelings are awesome.

Material wealth is no longer pride of place.
Every corner of your mind, you see her face.
Just longing for that contact first touch of her hand.
A love to last as long as our beaches have sand.

Meet, we touch, like static, strikes deep into your heart.
Knowing these feelings are from both we'll never part.
Why for some is this life so fulfilling, so good.
Alive once more with purpose, not misunderstood.

Never let a day of love slip through your fingers.
Make sure this precious feeling, a lifetime lingers.
Blessed your heart beats so fast, creating welcome pain.
Excitement of a child your new love takes her reign.

A good day in my heart for I know she is there.
Thank you my darling, thank you, for showing you care.
Grow old cosseting these feelings keeping them strong.
This world has wonders for us to share the day long.

Good morning my love, wishing a good day for you.
Open your eyes, see all that's great — life to ensue.
It's with all I have heart and soul, I make this wish.
An imaginary pond of love ~ yours to fish.

For all who LOVE AGAIN

Chapter Two

Grief Poems

This collection was produced from pain, at times as though someone were slowly pushing a knife into my stomach, twisting it, to point the tip straight back up towards my heart.
Yes wishing it were true, and the pain would end.

Slowly we learn to turn negative into positive and allow life to be lived again.

Anniversary Sorrow

Each and every year brings anniversary sorrow,
thoughts deep of yesterday, today and tomorrow.
I know you have left me, but still here in my mind,
I will continue to search, my lost love to find.

Anniversaries repeat, again and again,
continually bringing us so much heartache and pain.
Perhaps time to remember all the good over bad,
however hard I try, always seems that it's sad.

Our life together linked, so many celebrations,
since your departure, it is just consternation.
What's this life about, sets us up for this great fall,
seems the prime mover, is our final curtain call.

This, something for which we can never be prepared.
With a love so deep, I wish never to be shared.
Mortality now a subject for science and research,
some saying it should be, in the hands of the church.

Religion a subject has been far from my mind.
It's so strange grasping hope, to again be entwined.
This the time, thoughts circle above like birds of prey,
perhaps for us to meditate, demons to slay.

What is it that's so wrong, stirring faith in our heart?
Could give us inner strength, for our life to restart.
If questions were answered, by dearly departed,
most hope the answer to be get life restarted.

With events further away, as the years pass by.
Memory still strong, pain seems to fade, let out a sigh.
Anniversary sorrow, this pain, healed over time.
Listen the wind angel as she sends you a chime.

Yet to meet again

Science tells us a cure ... just a breath or two away,
not very helpful, when the cure we need today.
Disease touches all, least the ones we love, we know.
It is science we now need, a lifeline they can throw.

We are told that man's hand is not the hand of God.
So naked is the horse, until the horse is shod.
Riding the back of life, concealed from future ills,
once exposed and growing, causing so many spills.

Seemingly we've moved so far from 100 years ago.
When the reaper comes to reap, we just have to go.
Spirits have no substance, no material desire,
floating... infinity getting higher, yet higher.

Maybe that's where life departs, once this shell has gone.
For those who see the light, the light has always shone.
Those with blackness in their heart, life so full of doom;
white light spirits looking down, for them there's no room.

Redemption could be what they seek, a breath, a prayer;
with knowledge of your future, show him that you care.
We know man deep down, has capacity to forgive.
The days that we have left, a lifetime yet to live.

To think that this journey's made, disasters to avoid,
when touched with his scythe, there's no need to get annoyed.
Once we learn to embrace, how death forms part of life;
live each day seeing good, confronting all that's strife.

This human condition leaves us so frail, so weak.
Face the fear of death, of which most we never speak.
Embraced and understood, the end is not the end,
life beyond this life, where the good in us transcend.

Breathe her name

I awake and I breathe, breathe her name,
my head wise, heart consumed with love.
Rise from my slumber ... drowning man.
Lost to this world bound, yet alone.
Walk in her shadow, breathe her name,
everything gone nothing the same.
Dig deep, find reasons to live, exist.
Shadows on the wall take her shape,
still here, her presence feels so strong.
Touch her warmth, her lips still belong.
Existing, watch time ticking by
throughout the day, throughout the night.
Seen through eyes, a blackness no light,
my turn to go, my turn to die.
Whose decision, just tell me why?
So many, doing so much wrong.
Why choose the good, it's just not right.
Leaving us weak, unable to fight.
Search for reasons, searching for hope,
alone in this world, hard to cope.
Frailty exposed this vehicle we use,
mortality now enters our views.
Your loved one lived life, day by day,
wish now to take life, yours to slay.

Open your eyes, there are wonders to see,
under the surface you — are now she.

Gypsies of the Sea

As Life here ends, to be reborn,
spending time in grief, please don't mourn.

The plan I have, future for me;
become a Gypsy of the Sea.

Life full of hope, new world explore;
forget this shell I had before.

Roaming coast to coast, feeling free;
dolphins, "The Gypsies of the Sea."

If, you have seen them in their pods,
in their surroundings, they are gods!

Hunting together, when they can;
members of an exclusive clan.

Satisfied, it's time to delight;
playing, jumping, and taking flight.

Tail first, as they land with a splash ...
from the shore, you can hear, the crash!

Inside, they're laughing with us all;
dolphins live a life to enthral.

Once time's served in this great ocean,
angels wings, the next promotion.

Parallel Universe

Seems life can be cruel, seems life can be kind.
Parallel universe, when left behind.
Loved one departs, before canvas complete.
Left here to fight stand on our own two feet

We follow the road in body not mind,
Parallel universe for two – is kind.
Stumble and fumble try to find our way.
Open the curtains, let light in I pray.

Pain ... loss, moves in a mysterious way.
Sleep brings respite, but returns in the day.
Open our eyes in the hope it's a dream;
Brain tells us no, in our soul we just scream!

Human conditions, prepare us for pain.
Seems throughout our life, again and again;
We witness disaster, witness the last fall.
Nothing prepares us, for his final call.

In the midst of darkness, midst of despair.
Both family and friends, show that they care.
Supporting from distance, some in our face.
Rejected for reasons this – the last race.

Parallel universe full of love ... hate;
Fill bottles with love, hide hate in a crate,
Using love to spread goodness far and wide.
Shine goodness from above, let no one hide.

The key from our loss remember the good;
Catching, one thing hang on to it you should.
The foundation of life – built upon hope.
These deepest of feelings help us to cope.

Millions who pass and only do good.
Collect their spirits and use them like wood.
Eternal flame shining ... from coast to coast.
They who do good we remember the most.

Free Spirit

Constraint is our body, constraint is mind;
Our spirit is free, I think you will find.
It is free, to float, it is free, to glide,
By some it is seen, it can also hide.

Away from this shell, could our life begin
Be seen to be good, committing no sin
This a vision, I think of life's long plan,
It's your spirit achieves, if anything can.

Born to this world in this cumbersome shell
For some it's called heaven, for most it's hell
We lurch between good, we lurch between bad
Think we are happy, but mostly we're sad

In this great universe, it's gone in a blink
Those who do good, there's a lot more I think
To be plucked from the ground, ne'er achieve all
Floating with spirits, a masquerade ball

If this is the vision, this is the plan,
A ticket to ride, I need if I can.
Free my spirit, let me take to the sky
It's with all free spirits I want to fly

Someone who claims no religion or faith
It's both night and day, I live with your wraith
Each hour passes, brings me closer to you
Dreamt last night, it's with your spirit I flew

I'm told true love can happen, it's out there
I fear it so deeply why do I care
When it was cupid who drew that first bow
His arrow brought love, a seed it did sow

Try sharing that seed with more than just one
Feeling right feeling wrong, I know you hon
Your free thinking spirit, it would be kind
A second love you would want me to find

If this should happen, if this should take place,
My promise to you it won't be a race.
The person seen at the front of the queue
The rest of my life, will always be you

As Another Year Passes

Brain changes gear in the blink of an eye,
as another year passes, passes us by.
Grief some say is good, others it's bad,
so many mixed emotions we even get mad.
Now know as I'm navigating through life,
the speed it has gone since the loss of my wife.
Could be closer in death to join hands once again,
are these thoughts crazy or just insane.
Maybe, maybe once confusion starts to subside,
turn on the light stop trying to hide.
Unlock the doors step out into the rain,
it must be God's way to cleanse all of this pain.
Life whilst you live it, and clearly seen through your eyes,
is there to be lived, listen he cries.
Embark on adventures, an adrenaline rush,
heart and mind surely, feel the next crush.
Things done now are with little thought,
accelerator floored, fond memories to be taught.
First love resting in paradise under a tree,
with really clear views across the sea.
Looking down on us magnanimous in mind,
kindness within me, it's her you will find.
From afar she supports all that I do,
saying time to move on, be brave follow through.
Put down this grief time to pack it away,
open up your life, make the most of each day.
She sleeps on an island where dreams come true,
under a summery sky, best colour blue.
Gently placed by hands she knows and holds dear,
my love resting forever, she has no fear.
So take heed each morning when you awake,
see a glass that's half full, a new life to make.
Things that are worth having not handed on a plate,
meeting new folk just left up to fate.

The harder we look the more effort we make,
true love to be found, ensure it's not fake.
Sometimes it is instant heart shines through our eyes,
a loving relationship it now ties.
Like a perennial plant love just grows,
it gets stronger and stronger wriggling our toes.
Signs are there just need to look,
with the best of ingredients, all we need is a cook.
This being who mixes and bakes with flare,
his artwork complete, he now knows that you care.
Again to ride high, the white stallion of love,
sent for your pleasure from somewhere above.
Hold up your arms hands open and grab,
grasp tightly this feeling, for it can be just fab.
The capacity to love within us all to share,
each breath we now take, showing we care.
Surely life's meant to be lived, I will I must,
else leave this world trying, a vein will bust.
To bring joy to bring happiness, bringing a smile,
makes each day living really worth while.
I have reflected this year and many years past,
the luck iv'e had, and long may it last.
Conclusions iv'e reached at last meeting myself,
good fortune iv'e had including my health.
The knowledge we gain if we keep open minds,
there to help others I think you will find.
First born, into adulthood grow,
old age can be best if we believe it to be so.
This is the most difficult to convey,
remove all that's pain, let in laughter today.
Break our world up, much smaller pieces,
individuals effecting change, just increases.
Perhaps in the great scheme of things hard to compete,
in our little bit not such a feat.
Maybe dreaming big dreams, your circle of close friends,
positive thoughts and positive ends.

I Wonder

I sit, I wonder where they are;
all those, who've passed before.
Doth our soul float beyond the clouds?
If only all of us were sure.

To secure our lives here on earth,
to take away the pain.
Arms surround, gently comfort us,
a presence to remain.

Live in hope a higher power;
believing, without proof.
Early as a child, the fairy;
gently, collects your ~ tooth.

Father Christmas or Santa Claus;
that man all dressed in red.
But once a year delivers gifts;
whilst, you're asleep in bed.

Imagination running wild;
as, years so fast unfold.
Things that man clearly cannot stop,
as each, we all grow old.

There's many ways we meet our end;
sometimes, there is control.
For most it's preordained you see,
as the lion takes the foal.

We look to science, we must have proof;
There're things we cannot see.
Open minds now creative thought,
will help to set you free.

When love has struck each enters each,
our lives, to always bind.
Should one move to a higher plane,
a piece is left behind.

No you cannot see but you feel
your heart most every day.
It thumps and bumps because of them,
through you — they have a say!

Christmas Alone

Christmas time, comes and goes in the blink of an eye,
standing on a platform, as your train flashes by.
Some of us seem grateful, those who's soul is not lost,
In trepidation wait — to see our hearts defrost.
The struggle we undergo, battles in our mind,
it's not Christmas, we hate, it's loneliness you'll find.
When a hand is stretched out, to grasp a hand of ours;
our mind rejects it ... a vase of wilting flowers.
Is it fair the smile we smile, kept deep down inside;
holding a dark secret, we're trying hard to hide.
To some it's a joyous time, read it in their face
those living in the shadows, can't get past first base.
Christmas alone doesn't mean there is no one there,
can it be a state of mind — do we really care?
Both eyes need be opened, our hearts be opened too,
for the pleasure Christmas brings, love for me and you.
My observation, humanity, most we just cope,
from deepest depths of our soul, there is always hope.
Adjusting our approach, not difficult we find,
this shell of solitude ... or is it just our mind.
Accepting Lord Jesus Christ, travelled on a mule,
history's first jester, "you think he was a fool?"
The words we read in his book, sent here to redeem,
Christmas, commercialised, for mankind it would seem.
Perhaps we need to take a breath, readdress a thought,
happiness deep inside, cannot be really bought.
Let's step back, two for one, perhaps our minds to change,
if you've no human solace ~ HE's within your range.

Darkness

Days of darkness.
Days shining bright.
Days we made peace.
Days when we'd fight.

Unstoppable progress.
Till extinguished subdued.
Now laid to rest, more stress,
for me, and all who viewed.

Inner pain deep.
Sharp blade on skin.
Laying — a heap.
Wait to begin.

This journey without time.
Destination unknown.
Judged, committing no crime.
Mind been completely blown.

Wake a new dawn.
Eyes can they see.
A love to mourn.
Reflect — it's me.

All journeys have an end.
Promise, pain will subside.
Your heart begins to mend.
For you a life ~ unhide.

Light is the guide.
Remove the weight,
on life to glide.
Once again skate.

If I Should GO

If I should go tomorrow, just a thought or two.
It's my heart, I have left here, left with all of you.
Love constant stays forever, never says goodbye.
Teardrops kiss thy cheeks in sadness but please don't cry.

A love that flows to depths so deeply within me.
A gift for all please see 'tis a gift, given free.
Now radiates, envelops, glitters like the stars.
There to help I promise in healing all the scars.

The many wrongs that we do whilst this life we live.
Purged within our last breath, at last a chance to give.
Our final hope — above beyond all other hope.
Those are left live fully, with life they all can cope.

Now's time to reflect, not a time for being sad.
A life lived so completely, exits feeling glad.
Watching over from this place, yet unknown to man.
My last instruction is SMILE, for I know you can.

The Matriarch's Role

Inevitable consequence of life.
This shell borrowed, our soul we keep.
Cometh the moment we must rest.
Now and forever — her body to sleep.

There is no more discomfort no more pain.
She will always be by your side.
Life is full of much good, some bad.
She's lived her life well, and lived it with pride.

Her job here complete — the baton is yours.
The matriarch's role is now you.
Looking back over all these years;
time is, to reflect how quickly it flew.

Her message on the breeze so strong and clear.
We're not on this earth to rehearse.
We must make the best of each day.
Finding as much that is good, and immerse.

Feeling abandoned and left to make do
Think she will always be ~ a part of you

Chapter Three

Nature Poems

Perhaps, sometimes harnessed, but never tamed a thing of utter beauty and yet so much power. She will always be our master; her decisions can be and are often, final.

She can touch you with the delicacy of a new born child, she can rip your world apart. She is the inspiration for so many amazing works of literature and art, SHE IS!

Her Absolute Power

Makes man cower;
supreme power.
Wondrous, nature unfolds;
She will enchant ...
nurture a plant.
She allures, yet She scolds.

Gaze o'er the sea;
on it – feel free ...
Her absolute power.
Currents run wild ...
when calm – beguiled;
angry, She will devour.

Mountains doth build;
Man conquers — thrilled
beware, when they turn bad.
Seen it before;
now left in awe.
Revenge can leave us sad.

Stunning sunset ...
not to forget;
storms, will tear out your heart!
Rips through your world;
properties hurled ...
left to rebuild, restart.

Nature's a pearl;
watch Her unfurl ...
to cast Her magic spell.
She can amaze;
look on and gaze;
then, She takes you to hell!

Meekness and strength,
keep at arms' length ...
Nature, cannot be tamed.
She is this earth
and all its worth;
She's here to be — acclaimed.

Spring

The first blade of grass as it's sheered in spring,
that first breeze whistling, as birds start to sing.
First colour returns — our gardens ablaze;
first heady feeling, spring brings to amaze.

As the sun warms the soil, hearts start to glow,
most beautiful season things start to grow.
It's not just our gardens, sit up and prance,
when spring has sprung, it's our hearts start to dance.

Feelings of energy, bubble within,
plants in our gardens, new life to begin.
Perhaps we should measure lives by a year,
mistakes ... the past new beginnings no fear.

The heat of the sun's rays, she warms our flesh;
with nature as one, our world starts to mesh.
We could right all the wrong, man has to do,
first word of a child, listen for that coo.

There are things in this life, make our minds fly.
There are things in this life, just make us high.
There are things in this life, which cause us pain.
There are things — which will repair us again.

Calling on all, with hope, life she fulfills,
she can right all wrongs can mend all the spills.
Gaze ~ swaying fields of yellow daffodils,
surveying our future, yes with some thrills.

Wake with the right head on, all will be well.
with eyes open, see good — others to tell.
Nature brings vision, much we can savour,
switch to macro, do yourself a favour.

Many things bring us down, balanced by up.
Our capacity for life, just fill your cup.
Waking your senses in your heart to sing;
this season returns – time we all call spring.

The Majestic Oak

Where acorns ground,
oak trees are found,
fingers, touching – the sky!
His roots take hold
in ground so – cold;
beginnings small – dream high.

A sapling yearns...
views beyond – ferns.
Heading towards the light.
Once, grown above
look down with love.
Survive, he learns to fight.

The oak tree sings
as he adds rings,
majestic as he grows,
He's on his way...
hug a tree *day*,
our lives entwined, God knows!

He is a friend,
just will not bend,
gives breath to all... this air.
His life is ours...
sunshine – showers.
"Shout loud, "We must take care!"

As men we're wise;
there's no disguise...
we should ***value*** the tree.
They're strong they're bold;
our lives they hold,
supporting you and me!

Let's plant an oak,
for us – no joke,
there's children to be born.
As we give birth
upon this earth,
it's trees that we should — *mourn*.

Natures Wrath

Nature she's seen as extreme, beauty and horror.
Randomly raises her head, today – tomorrow;
Coloured deep red, beyond anything man can create.
When angered, killing, maiming, our race she can hate.

Whence was she born, nature's wrath, her origins from where.
Warm breeze rips to a cyclone, does she really care?
Rain brings and supports life, in a blink turns to floods;
Following days, the flowers all display their buds.

Snow paints pictures more creative than man can be;
An avalanche the power, sets so many free.
Calm seas greet us, like maidens beckon a lover.
Rip-tides... waves whisk us away, never to recover.

Lives lost in the heat of the sun, thirst leads to death.
Cold and ice, the North-Pole, a need to catch one's breath.
Her power, every corner of this planet pries.
Man yet to fathom, she decides who lives, who dies.

Tectonic plates moving, friction, eventually break;
Ground above, feeling the force, what we call a quake.
Knowledge is what we need or she will always win.
In awe the strength she wields, begin a new, begin

She gives or takes a life, in the blink of an eye.
Freedom crossing borders, most people left to cry.
Her way to maintain balance – population control.
Wish all the good she brings, inspired us to enrol.

This echo system, intelligent we believe.
These horrors maybe planned, planned for us to relieve.
Pressures that we build up, from our petulance ... greed.
Our constant quest to survive, fulfill wants not needs.

Must come a time, the penny will finally drop.
What our world has, and gives is not an open shop.
Saturation's no option, for man to survive.
Control numbers for our species, to stay alive.

Intoxicating Fragrance

Intoxicating fragrance with such beauty for us — to see.
English gardens can be there for all, or just for you and me.
As ninety hyacinths in unison rear their heads in pride.
From invigorating stimuli there's nowhere we can hide.

Once dying back the goodness always returning to the bulb.
Now the turn of the fragrant cherry tree, us to all behold.
The perfumed herbs, the lilac's splendour and its delicate smell.
Garden so full of scent, and colour consumed you have to tell.

Plan each border with forethought maximise both colour, and scent.
Once one has been and gone for the next to please, you are hell bent.
With much research to find the plants that match your every whim.
A desire to blow all minds, and senses — impact, make them swim.

In wonderment they all will be, once your plants achieve these heights.
I know they all will come from far and wide just to catch these sights.
The bonus without doubt will be the attack upon their nose.
There will be times it is so strong, it will crinkle up their toes.

Our senses have been given us to tantalise play, and feel.
Things that cross the peripheries, striking more than one appeal.
It's clear gardening needs abundant creative skills, and more.
Just like any art form when it's right will thrill us to the core.

Once the soil is warm, ready to grow nurture its next delight.
Spending time, pick and choose those flowers the senses to excite.
Like all works of art our creations are really good to share.
When there is only one to please, in wonderment you still care.

It is your hope that boundaries between those from here depart.
Still capturing all this beauty, from the depths of our own heart.
Good memories, important to our soul even when they're sad.
Reminiscence helps us getting through, turning our mood to glad.

This love of life captured, in all that we experience, we feel.
Not all the things that touch us, our scientists confirm are real.
For those that are on a mission, to expose all that feels great.
Removing that is considered bad — to take away mans hate.

Gardens have these qualities a place for fun, and to relax.
There're many open that we can view, which on our brain impacts.
Piece by piece for us to bring home, recreating in your back yard.
Those so fortunate to have this space, promise it is not hard.

Chapter Four

Heston Blumenthal

Channel 4, ran a four part series with Heston, using his unique culinary skills to improve both the quality, and flavour of food being served in NHS Alder-hay, British Airways, Cineworld, and The Royal Navy submarines.

These programmes were a joy to watch, and gave the inspiration for the four poems that follow.

Mission Impossible

Alder Hey, Liverpool, children's hospital trust.
Improving the menu, use Heston it's a must.
He lives his life at pace ever chasing that rush.
Ingredients he mixes, and spices he must crush.

Food sparks imagination, excites like a child.
Presentation important got to drive them wild.
Caterpillar Pizza, and don't forget the worms.
This is a hospital, HB, beware of the germs.

You've got to try vomit soup, or even snot shake.
This fun and adventure your palates will awake.
The food that we're eating will help us to improve.
HB's menu full of fun, sad faces will remove.

Breaks down prejudice, a politician you see.
Accepting his Mission Impossible, on our TV.
For some many changes are very hard to bear.
Stand back aghast, accept your menu, not a prayer.

The Fat Duck his retreat when he's needing to think.
Success or failure, with his career on the brink.
Watching all those kids faces, success it must be.
He must convince them, innovation is the key.

Perhaps a sad inditement, the place that we live.
We're dragged kicking and screaming, before we can give.
On second thoughts for most of us, our time spent blind.
When shown the light within us, our thoughts can be kind.

Talent is a gift few hone, seeking perfection.
For those who do, stay steady, maintain direction.
They're examples to us all, these folk who can win.
The HB's of this world, show others where to begin.

Once on that road be firm, for work you can enjoy.
Dig deep, find some strength, your management to annoy.
They say thinking laterally, that's not lying down.
Watch the children's faces, as they smile with the clown.

Cineworld

His next impossible challenge – in our cinema,
to excite our senses, maybe one step... far.
Failure, expected from the management team.
Heston and his boys, produce a fairground dream.

Cineworld's brave decision, show profits galore.
Stephen, the MD, who runs it, not from this shore.
Their prime objective you see must produce wealth.
Some of these snacks are not so good for our health.

Our brave champion, Heston, now faces his quest.
He's got flavours to make you eat your own vest.
Cooked in liquid nitrogen gives it a crunch;
you'll request seconds, as on that vest you munch.

What's it, that's so difficult to understand.
Added value, will give you the upper hand.
Punters aren't stupid, experiencing this change.
loyalty and support, they will try the whole range.

Hotdogs to die for, being served inside out;
even eat the wrapper, listen to them shout.
Ice-cream made from popcorn, tasting just sublime.
Suspense increased as the public wait in line.

Smell seems a sense when added to sight and sound,
enhances food, in all cinemas around.
Watching numerous programmes where he's used this,
seems from observation, that it is just bliss.

Now my hope, our hero, Heston will prevail.
Whatever the challenge, through rough seas to sail.
The ambience this team have designed to be used.
Brings back the fun, they enjoy and are amused.

My hope is this team will set up a supply,
made easy to cook and serve, not to deny.
Cash can be made from adventures of this sort.
Don't waste creative skills, don't just press abort

Air borne

Heston's next impossible challenge is setting a new goal.
British Airways with many routes— planes and staff to control.
Decide to look more closely, at the food on these flights served.
Our hero called for fresh ideas, must throw a ball that's curved.

Training before you take flight, let's see you push this trolley;
a duck to water, our friend becomes — A "Trolly Dolly."
Heston demonstrates, that infamous cabin crew wiggle.
Teachers both standing there unable to hold back a giggle.

His inaugural flight leaves nowt but food for thought of course.
All his knowledge and experience, ideas he must not force.
Change can be made much easier when they are all on your side.
Key to acceptance, problem exist, whoops this food is dried.

Gate Gourmet the largest air kitchen, whose food it takes flight.
Supplying meals for British Airways, through the day and night.
Steve head chef, worried for his job, with Heston there he squirms.
Whatever done, please don't include, snail porridge, even worms.

As he prods he pokes, it's knackered, it's oxidised, it's grey.
Pre-cook the answer, this food's been cooked twice to death I pray.
Passengers seem resigned, once in the air, all food tastes bad.
Preconception our hero must change, makes him really mad.

A Herculean challenge if it wasn't, would've been done before.
Back and forth to Bray, find a way to get up from the floor.
Moisture seems just one problem, a nasal douche served with food.
Strangers sitting beside me, snorting, afraid would be rude.

One big key to moving forward, convince Steve this is real.
An altitude chamber, blindfold, taste flavours for the meal.
Like walking in a room that's dark, then being shown the switch.
Our head chef at last can see ways for his food, to enrich.

All our ducks in a row, now's time to come up with a dish.
A shepherd's pie we hear him say, no way could it be fish.
Now there's a secret ingredient, Heston wouldn't let us down;
Seaweed you wouldn't believe it, for this pie it adds a crown.

Once again our hero has risen, slowly to the top.
His shepherd's pie, not just accepted, praised by all, full stop.
His next impossible challenge, with intrigue we await.
Confident that, Heston's futures not in the hands of fate.

All at Sea

The captain's comments, your country needs you Mr B.
Your next impossible challenge, sending you to sea.
It's not on the surface, that you'll perform this task.
Panic not, things go wrong, you'll have an oxygen mask.

Adrenaline rush kicks in, sleeping in a hive.
Bed partner, a live missile, tends to sleep deprive.
On second thoughts could be worse, barrel comes to mind.
In those days, no coming out, watch your own behind.

It's up for breakfast, the full Monty they all share.
Our hero it's so stodgy, for them do they care.
Tracking radar, a job required to be alert.
Food, the oxygen of our soul, with the devil flirt.

King's College, the answer, ingredients won't fail.
Keeping his shipmates with a bright and bushy tail.
That awful porridge, I think they called it Bagoo.
Had one serious ending, poured it down the loo.

This impossible challenge goes way beyond the norm;
Space a major problem, with those on board lukewarm.
With Heston and all his friends, focused on the case.
We know there is an answer, they will win this race.

Similar problems – exist within the forces.
Everyone needs to eat, eureka hold your horses.
Pre-cook and shrink wrapping, giving his food the edge.
The navy's top brass, now giving Heston a pledge.

Once again my friend you are on the winning team.
They all now see this challenge, ending up a dream.
These years now have passed, restricting active duty.
Answers they now have, better than – tutti-fruity

Our hero and his team, a deserved sense of pride.
Visually it's obvious his emotions cannot hide.
He makes it clear on camera, feelings running high.
With many great achievements, this one hits the sky.

Chapter five

Protest Poems

Throughout ones life you meet injustice, or your interpretation of injustice. Where you can, you must express those emotions; not all of us feel the same about things and that is what makes us human.

So this section is there to create debate, those who agree join with me, those who disagree fight your corner.
Those who sit on the fence, do a Humpty Dumpty, if it's my side you fall you will be repaired.

War what for?

I hear people say what is this state called war, to fight to kill "oh what for?"
Wealthy countries from around the globe, even those in ecclesiastical robe.
Battle cry they all give, the worlds requirement, "peace," will allow all to live.
Seems it is blood that's on their mind, no real thought for how it effects mankind.

Some from children with a zest to fight, by killing others doesn't make it right.
Our leaders on whom we rely, take us to war don't listen to our cry.
Playground posturing my dad's better than yours, no he's not, mine hit six fours.
Take time out time to learn, to seek, understanding feelings, that make us weak.

This aggression is born to help survive, doesn't always help, keep us alive.
Used by our peer group, tap into this well, decisions made, take us to hell.
For those... decide to take us to war, include them, would ask, "what for?"
There's some born to think, some to do, those going to war will always be you.

Look at reasons — take us to war, is it conviction, or settle a score?
Just stop, think a while, where would they go, if we all stood up, we all said no.
There is one thing of which I have no doubt, left up to them, most would cop out.
Wealth and power are spoils they need, to achieve this end they will watch you bleed

This a message well worth giving, remember the dead, protect the living.
To the ends of the earth we'd go, before allowing people's blood to flow.
Use all of our knowledge, power and might; make the decision not to fight.
Minds can change clarity of thought, togetherness agreement, must be sought.

NO MORE WAR NO MORE WAR NO MORE WAR NO

Confusion fear as you stand alone, is this weakness or strength, seeds you've sown.
Sense says snowdrops melt in your hand, avalanche more difficult to withstand.
Message required to take from this place, it's talking we need, to save our race.
Lessons I know are hard to be taught, review all the wars man's ever fought.

Once proof war's the only way in the end, views I promise I will amend.
With passion soul deep down my hope, removal of wars to see us all cope.
Wealth released able to spend, improving conditions, for all in the end.
Surely possible— we've got to try, remove this evil, wave it goodbye!

Medals

Step forth for GLORY, can this be true;
For, to war is where they're taking you.
Honoured whilst you're watching other's backs.
Shedding blood and kill for medals.
Lessons taught whilst young are now abandoned;
Survival, try to keep your limbs.
Messages "wrong to scrap" instilled when young.
Confused – opposite now to fight,
higher powers say... "it's now alright."
Take up your weapon, aim and shoot.
A competition set by them, kill or be killed.
Decorations pinned upon your chest.
Enemies lay dying, blood stains on their vest.
In this mayhem lives are lost;
People, born to live have to die – what cost.
Man makes these decisions best;
Confirmation, seeing medals on your chest.
Awarding medals ~ calms your mind;
Home, resting in your bed it's <u>NO</u> you'll find.

Born to fall

Are we born to fall, surely not to save.
For some, it is power they seek.
For most, here just once, they forever crave.
Yet concrete gains, still leave us weak.

As the richness of life, grows from inside;
it is few, who have that power.
Radiate the sparkle of life, the pride,
spend their lives, living hour by hour.

Without wealth, can be incredibly rich,
it's not something you just acquire.
Many with money, do anything to switch,
this natural gene, leaves one higher.

Average we now live, three score years and ten.
My message "All are born to fall."
So many lives lived, wish to live again.
Leave we must, when we get that call.

Perhaps nature's way, give others a chance,
growing, a child's not about gain.
Once new children are born, through life to prance.
Material wealth also brings pain.

Giving all our children, reason for hope,
understanding, they're born to fall.
Able to live lives, not having to cope.
Make the best... exceptionally cool.

Learning to love both, the pleasures, the joy.
Bountiful new things every day.
Free to experience, engage don't be coy.
When time to fall, most's done, can say!

Some live at the most incredible speed.
Not measured by years, not measured by greed.

Locked - in Syndrome

My family have lost me the damage already done.
My life living through others now, not so much fun.
Each morning awakening, with pain in my heart,
this shell now worthless, it's time to let it depart.

What is it with mankind, always think they know best,
never having lived in this shell, they wouldn't invest.
Just one of the things we should have for free, is choice.
Then, "time to go" I'd shout! from the top of my voice.

Please help, what is it, the majority have to do?
Break the hold of the minority, just think it through.
I agree ... most precious thing in this world is life.
Scream, "dignity!" for me departing from my wife.

Living like a vegetable only eyes can see,
when reflected in a mirror, please set me free.
We have a kind side, when animals are in pain,
medical intervention now acts, no refrain.

This burden I have placed on my family and friends,
will now colour their view, memories in the end.
This burden now placed on our system, yes for cash.
When at every twist and turn, budgets being slashed.

Please I beg — respect my wishes, now is my time.
Life holds little meaning to take it, is no crime.
Allowing people loved to move on, just to live.
With little left please don't deny this thing, I give.

Locked-in syndrome mustbe experienced first hand,
For those have not been there, and just don't understand.
Hear — Nicklinson is my name, Tony to my friends.
My fight's for freedom, this prison release, intend.

Its fate that has for some reason, now locked me in,
whatever faced, could be my future to begin.
Should this not be the case the legacy left behind,
allow freedom, **CHOICE**, in the end for all mankind.

Aftercare

Took a panic phone call this morning from an elderly aunt.
Sped round to her place in top gear I would not say, "I can't!"
Very clear she needed help, so an ambulance was called.
The speed that they arrived amazed, left only to applaud.

The journey to hospital — quick, it was at mega speed.
The Doctors working on her were just great, we all agreed.
Then downhill it goes from here, things going from bad to worse.
The way she was treated, I would rather have called a hearse.

What is the point of all that time spent trying to save life.
Aftercare does not exist; you're just causing us more strife.
She waits on a gurney; sixteen hours spent in her own pee.
Not once were her blankets changed, giving a little dignity.

First waiting for a bed seemed just hours, finally to be told,
one's become available, but afraid it's been put on hold.
Only have three working porters transporting all our sick.
This person manages these men, afraid he's just a p---k.

Would like to know his take home pay, bet he is living well.
From distance, all he does is point, perhaps should do a spell.
If he were to see the frustration caused, the living hell.
Could be this pointing digit, a wand, helping problems quell.

It seems we are laden with bureaucrats women and men.
Paid more than enough to expect decisions now and then.
If you're not poised to follow through adding quality to life,
forget seven years you have spent learning to use a knife.

Me — I would rather have a scientist produce a pill,
for me to take swallow, should ever I become too ill.
Think of all the money this would save in medics needed,
Bet your bottom dollar this message will go unheeded.

Here surely is a simple cry, from all, who this have faced.
Those who are well paid, and have the power, please do not waste.
Once the hard bit completed, and a life is saved, secured.
Have pride in things you have done, and the quality you've assured.

Final Choice

For some of us this decision, not ours to take.
It's the medical professions, one they will make.
The oath that is sworn, life at whatever the cost.
The end of the day — our dignity they have lost.

There are times when it is taken out of their hands.
Some say our road is fate, others, celestial plans.
I know from experience and all that I have seen,
so many are affected, their life to demean.

When you tread life's path with a love one who's distressed;
what you're getting told, it's with your heads they have messed.
Questions galore erupt from the depth of your mind.
What you need is answers, it's not answers, you find.

Climbing vertical walls, nails stretching for a hold.
Taking life day by day, thoughts in your mind are bold.
Negative doesn't exist, not a word you can use.
Hard, difficult times, it's always life that you choose.

Whatever thrown, how difficult it is to catch.
An inner strength will always find a way to match.
Things beyond the source of life, not to lose your grip.
Anything can be done, life in your favour to tip.

For most who go through this, take time out to reflect.
Loved one or your partner, please try not to reject.
This pain that they all suffer, both yours and their own.
A future without you that is barren — unknown.

The base of this subject, difficult it may be.
When you leave your body, it's you that is set free.
For those that are left behind, time to catch a breath.
Pain and tears grieving, for a love one and their death.

Guess what I'm saying, final choice should hold respect.
A choice made from knowledge, within the law and checked.
A decision covers all, allows informed choice.
My hope those that can, listen, to the peoples' voice.

59

The Boy Within

The boy within the man is free
Look very closely and find me

Although throughout the years we grow
Those visions kept, from long ago

Remembered too the days gone by
It is not hard, if you'll just try

It seems we would be out all day
From dawn to dusk, we all would play

Not ever once did we know fear
Despite the dangers lurking near

Our parents' call was always key
We all would run in for our tea

Our plates were emptied in a flash
And out to play once more we'd dash

It seemed that darkness fell too quick
That goal we need just one more kick

Each day was filled with so much fun
The weapons used just a toy gun

The man has grown how do you feel
For now the weapons used - are real

Destruction

Pray what are we doing to this planet where we live,
Our children who inherit, will they ever forgive?
We have raped and pillaged most of its mineral wealth.
Completely disregarding the effect on its health.

We procreate in places where life stands not a chance.
While others spend their leisure time at a disco dance.
One thing we have in common, yes all around this globe.
Most who have the power, have worn an academic robe.

Education's twist, teaches worship power — success.
Leave the masses to worry, leave them to second guess.
In the great scheme of things, it can only be short term.
Keeping people in the dark, creates a turning worm.

Moving their wealth from land to land, looking to secure
A life that they are now used to, may be premature.
Once turning worms have turned, surely there is no way back.
For they are many — nowt to lose who will just attack.

Lessons for our leaders, from all corners of this world.
However strong the surface from office can be hurled.
When pushing people that bit far, little have to lose
What you have known as support, the opposite they'll choose.

It's said there are none so blind as those who cannot see.
Yet is there a plan without support from you and me.
They want to think longer term, secure life on this earth.
Compromise — a word used, for spiritual rebirth.

Moving from material things there is value in love.
Something that must come from within, not from up above.
Let's hope this decision will be made — put into place.
Could put us back on track, help to save our human race.

Destruction, such a final word portrays no way back.
Somehow with kindness that I know in our favour stack.
It's that thing called balance, to which all must now subscribe.
Share fairly, we human beings are all ~ from one tribe.

Chapter six

Social Comment Poems

Observation one of our greatest assets, interpretation again is individual. The good, the bad and the ugly, words can be used like swords, strike and cut, they are also there to soothe and repair.

Do hope this section does a little of both.

Cat Woman

Women the gentler sex, we would expect to find.
Not always the case you see, some can be — unkind.
Nurture and nature, ways for bringing out the good,
If women were put in charge, lots believe they should.

Nowadays look close, there seems to be another side.
A catty streak, scratch and claw, then draw back and hide.
Competing with the men, reaching heights, hear their lies.
Looking closely stop and stare — see it in their eyes.

Use words to cut and slash their victims like a whip,
Some a kinder weapon, a six gun on the hip.
Leaving us to squirm with fear, have they too sold out.
Women who now replace men, what's that all about?

We have an expectation somehow they're the best,
Leaving us to crash and burn, they're just like the rest.
Jockey into position, strive... gain the upper hand.
Love, we've come to expect, is written in the sand.

For those who can, now is time just to stop and think.
Raise a glass to those you've hurt, offering a drink.
An olive branch you'll bring, it's not with which to beat,
But putting right all that's wrong, this is no mean feat.

The saying that, "cream will always rise to the top."
This is something cat woman, would not want to stop.
My hope is togetherness, we all live as one.
Surely so much better, vision our future ~ fun.

Dad

What is a dad but a figurehead, hanging from a boat.
His main purpose always was, to keep his family afloat.
At least in my time as a dad we knew that this was true,
Two thousand twelve it seems, a dad has so much more to do.

Emancipated women, struggle to become the man;
it is only evolution, will show if they really can.
Change we know they say is for good, it also can be sad.
Whatever will we do, when the kids start calling Mum, Dad.

This world surely has gone crazy, simple seems, now so wrong.
Experiments taking place, it's the man who wears the thong.
PC he was always dressed in blue, he served the law for good.
Now it's things minorities impose, do we think they should?

Confusion then begins to set in, when she's the hired gun.
Procreation for a man still strong, he also needs some fun.
No longer quite knowing, what's expected, what is his role;
Reverting back to cave man days and going on the dole.

Many young men are now confused, not sure of time or place.
For all their guile and cunning they will never reach first base.
It's said often by so many, that this is a man's world.
Now for sure, this direction changed, has out the window hurled.

All these things are taking place let us reach a conclusion.
Life as we know it, our future, becomes an illusion.
When we spend so much time focused, supporting dying breeds.
Perhaps we need look closer to home, some of mankind's needs.

Toy with life, make changes wholesale, with complete disregard.
Could I say, leave our human race, forever badly scarred.
There's nothing wrong with asking, discussion should go down well.
For man's worst enemy is a woman who can only tell.

So the case now for man is complete and I hope is strong.
Men now listen, we must communicate to get along.
Take some time to chat, help support a father's view on life.
For a child **mum** will stay a **mum**, for man ~ **a loving wife**.

Bad News Day

When living in this land of make believe,
the world and it's troubles easy to grieve.

Indeed seems wherever you turn your glance,
we're besieged by bad news, left in a trance.

Suffering souls tormented, torn apart,
every which way, appealing to your heart.

Please give generously, your soul redeem.
"Who do we leave out?" I can hear you scream.

Many say charity begins at home,
could say they're still living in a glass dome.

Afraid when seeking just what to give up,
many small things, perhaps that champagne cup.

We stretch our fingers, take care of this world,
thoughts of the suffering, toes it has curled.

Starting point would be, corruption remove,
powerful people whose lives we improve.

Now austerity, free income is the past,
thinking more clearly, donations must last.

Charity required, it's proof we all need,
sure it's purpose, not those living on greed.

Clear, the difference, 'tween have and have nots,
called generosity, for them drawing lots.

Answer yes, give, we're on this world to share.
A common theme through our race, most still care.

Unfortunately, all days bring bad news,
it's peoples response helps colour our views.

Bad news reversed is good, good goes down well,
come on people help ring that good news bell.

Chasing Shadows

Life is a bitch,
Always a hitch.
Never achieve – your goal.
"Look," I would say,
Most every day;
Search deep within your soul."

Your challenge new,
Your mood is blue.
Spent chasing shadows blind.
Never enough,
Physical stuff.
Your life has been declined.

Misplaced the route,
Turn-off the mute.
All can hear you crying.
Fools' gold (the dream),
When it would seem.
Inside – we are dying.

Perhaps a view,
From someone new,
Might help you find your way.
When clear, you know,
Inside aglow;
Directions, mere child's play.

At last you see,
In front of thee,
A map is now in hand.
A step each day,
Future convey.
Your time to come is grand.

Your wealth is near,
Your love revere.
Keep it simple, keep it free.
Sleep tight tonight;
Please, don't take fright,
For all is good – you see!

NOW?

Today it's all NOW, things to be done,
It doesn't happen NOW, life's not begun.
If there's something we want, it is NOW.
We all have a card, called a cash cow.
Pay for it why? When we have plastic;
Paying back, they promise they're elastic.
Like anything you bounce down to our toes,
Just comes back up, hits you on the nose.
How strange, things we want and do not pay,
Comes back, haunts us all — another day.
Please be aware the scene is now set,
For many folk to get into debt.
A short while you're living on a cloud,
I beg just listen, for you, stay proud.
Don't get caught in a lifestyle of spend;
Admit you must pay back in the end.
A life lived in a culture of greed.
It's only meant for a few, to feed.
Please open your eyes, see the result.
Put spending to bed, just call a halt.
You would find those who have would quiver;
Not long, before their spine will shiver.
Repercussions for us there would be,
From this word debt, all would be set free.
Thrifty an old fashioned word revive,
Begin a new begin to survive.
There is plenty we can have for free;
Richness, to be found for you and me.

Tick Tock

Time ticks by at a constant speed.
Think, the stamina it must need.
Seconds endlessly ticking by;
minutes, in the blink of an eye.
Minutes add to five and then ten,
process grinds, again and again.
Before we know, clock strikes the hour,
in the corner sit — we cower.
Stop for a rest, certainly not,
a constant pace, for all it's got.
Reach it's intention, reach it's end.
All mankind it's never a friend.
This objective, all of it's own;
reach twenty four, know it has grown.
It's a miracle, starts once more,
secs, mins, hours, reaches twenty four.
As days pass, they lead to a week,
whoever invented time — freak!
Month quickly turns to twelve, year gone.
River flows, watch a gliding swan.
Reflect not people time has passed,
look the future conquered at last.
Control of time — have if we can,
think what we need, carefully plan.
Waste not want not, it will pass quick;
listen intent, hear the clock tick.
You'll not catch it, use it with care,
set your ambitions, time to share.
Soon your batteries will run dry,
find next morning you've learned to fly.
A separate realm, you now move,
time still there, it's own little groove.
This small ditty's moral my friend,
whatever ~ time wins in the end.

Mother Earth

Mother Earth, this special globe, where all we live,
things we need to survive, she will freely give.
We have a duty to her, contract of care,
those living on this earth, be helpful and share.

In the last sixty years we've expanded at will,
moving without thought from two, to six point eight "bill".
Resources on this planet, fast becoming thin.
We damage our eco system, we just can't win.

Look, we're speeding blindly towards a brick wall;
believe, those who have most, take the biggest fall.
Some people must live on less, just one hectare;
higher standards others have, nine is that fair.

We MUST think, how many people live on this earth.
Before realising resources, there is a dearth.
There are those who know, there's a need to really share.
So many give little thought, in fact just don't care.

I have felt uneasy for some time without fact.
Sir David A tells us, it's time we must act.
Heading towards capacity this sphere will stand,
all must do something, in each and every land.

China has set the standards, one couple one child.
Introduce it to the world, would just drive them wild.
How else can we arrest this Kamikaze approach;
to balance earth's resources, for all no reproach.

Water soon will be the source of all our wars.
Scars left on this planet, never healing sores.
There is as much now as when the earth began;
it is there for all of life, not just for man.

We're constantly talking of the dangers we face;
overpopulation now, for our human race.
Mother Earth cannot manage, she's unable to cope.
This message needs be loud, clear, bringing us some hope.

What If!

What if we could unsay, take back when we have hurt someone.
What if once fired, remorse called the bullet back to the gun.
What if three little letters which make WAR did not exist.
What if anger in our mind, didn't cause cascades of red mist.
What if the weakest beings, were protected by the strong.
What if all could tread with confidence, in this world belong.
What if a higher power, shadowed us all on this crust.
What if all held the same belief, saying love... peace, a must.
What if these feelings, we captured and held for just a while.
What if looking into people's eyes, you could see them smile.
What if this a template, for all future generations.
What if these are seeds been sown, awaiting germination.
What if this world could live as one, seeing all that is good.
What if for most of us, What if, What if, we really could.

The Pen

A poet writer's pen
reveals all .
It peels back the skins;
layer by layer.
Like an onion exposing
its inner self.
Tears run down cheeks;
fun, sadness.
To moisten parchment,
to express.
To reveal nakedness,
expose soul.
Immortality it seeks,
indelibly.
A creative masterpiece,
to find.
Serving entertaining,
mankind.

The Journey

Rising, seven springs unite bringing life to see.
Meandering, caressing banks, nooks and crannies,
Glides over familiar rocks, remembers old friends.
His constant journey begins once more, to give birth.
Had he known, memories he would evoke the life.
The willow weeps as its fingers break his surface.
No map required, he follows a preordained route;
No mortal man remembers, but from archives seen;
Imprisoned, within his own banks he can break free.
Gently flows tasting smatterings of salt he knows.
Man tries to tame and use him, but their lives are his.
For those with depth, who reflect their souls, they can see;
Surface, a mirror image under flesh reveal.
In his depths mysteries of bygone years are held.
In his body trout dance whilst others just pass through.
Glories of man placed strategically to impress;
What lasts the test of time, buildings or that river?
Relentless, push forward, cat hunting on dry grass;
almost silent, in pursuit of his end purpose.
That taste of salt, tantalising, marks his journeys end.
Obstacles and bridges he passes with such stealth.
The open sea his goal, through estuary to pass,
They meet, they touch, they blend, they reunite at last.
Always to return, to those rising seven springs.

The Blade

For all those whose pain clearly worn upon their sleeve;
Ensure a sharpened dagger, ne'er drawn from its sheath.
Legend says, "once the blade is flashing in the sun."
A strike must be made, someone's blood has got to run".
Be wary friend, things get hot, tempers start to boil.
Your heart has little defence – to this cold steel foil;
Disputes rampant around this globe, emotions flare.
When anger moves beyond sense, things we do aren't fair.
The pain we bring, to this world in the name of pride;
Looking down upon your sleeve, you just want to hide.
Damage now has been done, the blade has done its job;
A life gone, for them no hope, in your soul you... sob.
Years to come on your back, burden you must carry;
What will seem eternity, sorrow deep will tarry.
Albeit this pain you wear, clear upon your sleeve;
Innocence of youth now gone, left for you to grieve.

Cordon Bleu

A poem, like a meal, needs thought;
this, a talent that can be taught!

First, your subject for this is key;
seek interest for all who see.

Your menu, which is now in place;
think quality, this is no race.

Ingredients, you pluck a word;
to catch the sound of a song bird.

Cordon Bleu chef you want to be;
yet, mix and cook like a trainee.

Take time now, your poem rehearse;
as you construct it, verse by verse.

Presentation is in your head;
punctuation, a thing you dread.

Steadfast, attack have got to try;
complete this project do or die.

I face the penultimate fence,
and all I've used is common sense.

Displaying work before I post;
keep it simple, and do not boast.

Time

Time a commodity we just cannot buy,
powerful and wealthy continually try.
Their gains are just futile of this I am sure,
it is not for sale on a stock exchange floor.

Time has great value it is honest and fair,
wherever we meet him for all he will share.
Class disregarded rich or poor, strong or mild.
Whatsoever your status – even a child.

Time has more value than any mineral wealth,
it is given for free, some wish it were health.
Knows no barrier, classless crossing nations.
Squandered or creating amazing sensations.

Seems no one can stop it, hard as they might try.
With all of our knowledge it just seems to fly.
Time is more precious, than this so called black gold.
Time the enigma – that we just cannot hold.

Day commences, quickly ticks by and is gone.
Our moods can effect it when sunshine has shone.
Time can be our enemy, can be our friend.
One thing to be sure its still there at the end.

Wandering through time, searching yourself to find.
True that you haven't – left someone else behind.
You are you, with knowledge surely to improve.
There's no point in trying yourself to remove.

Realities playing its part in your life,
accept time as a free gift, not to cause strife.
Grasp it with both hands please use it to fulfill.
Time allowing humans – the freedom to thrill.

Best Friends

Best friends stretch borderlines can include hope.
Heavy burdens – it's best friends help us cope.
Best friends stretch boundaries cross species too.
Your best friend is someone means most to you.

It's not I don't know you... just haven't met.
It's not I don't know you... not spoken yet.
Universe decided you're my best friend.
Heard someone saying it's fate in the end.

All I'm asking is come be my best friend.
Enemies will slay you not your best friend.
Trust sometimes becomes love with your best friend.
All emotions are shared with your best friend.

Once you have bonded there's no going back.
Nights out on the town you will have a crack.
One drink leads to two, could be three, then four.
Next thing that we know, picked up from the floor.

This invitation goes out far and wide,
Real friends can be precious help turn the tide.
It's to friends we turn, supporting our needs,
It's to friends that we turn and their good deeds.

A best friend is priceless, adds more than wealth;
Life full of warnings, not bad for your health.
Best friends often outlast time and beyond;
Found... locked into, forming chemical bonds.

GOLD

Once awake inspired, step up to the plate;
some days we love, yet there are some we hate.
Measured by standards, which are set by man,
all strive to win if they possibly can.
For many the bar has been set too high,
their zest to achieve will too quickly die.
For a few now, this passion burns inside;
success the beacon, to success applied.
For all those now wishing, they wore those shoes.
These heroes, mere Gods, we see never lose.
They sit, on the top of our pedestal,
from dizzy heights, it's a long way to fall.
As they cross the line first, this world they hold;
standing top of the rostrum, they've got GOLD.

This Olympics

Summer, two thousand twelve begins;
our sporting heroes, see who wins.

London England, now on the map;
tourists' cameras, catch that snap.

A feast of sport that's now on show;
for all to watch it, blow by blow.

Years of training in their own sport,
competition, they try to thwart.

The ultimate reward is, gold!
In their hands, they each want to hold.

The world all gathers those who care;
this Olympics for all to share.

Those watching and those taking part,
excitement builds before the start.

Ceremonies now days away,
"God keep all safe" is what I pray.

They have arrived to do their best;
proud nations' colours on their vests.

When this sporting bonanza ends,
its main purpose - to create friends!

How would it make you feel

The damage done when our brain's not in gear,
the things that we say, are things they now fear.
Words said out of place, so easily destroys,
consider feelings, they're human – not toys.

Think, be careful, when making a new friend,
be caring ... loving don't judge in the end.
This shell we carry is there for the ride;
It's what's underneath, it's what is inside.

We can so easily cause, blackness of mood;
so many cases, it's just being rude.
Leave a soul deep down in depths of despair;
If you were this person, would it be fair?

Trapped ... cocoon of loneliness left to cry
cut and hurt deeply — with a wish to die.
Respectful think, "How would it make you feel?"
Reflecting it's time that you can now heal.

When you're judging another don't misperceive
Ensure all of your facts, please don't be naive
Walk tall on this soil be proud to be kind.
Returned by like-minded others – you'll find.

The Brigade

Here to protect children, husbands, and wives.
Our role in this world — is help saving lives.
Shifts are spent in wait for danger to strike.
Once that bell rings, we are all on our bike.

The lessons we are taught from the first day.
Work as a team, our commanders obey.
Discipline you know felt key to our task.
Aptitude to detach, wear anyone's mask.

Situations seen throughout our career.
Bring the strongest of us to shed a tear.
Call upon humour, to get past first base,
Help and guide us in the dangers we face.

We form family bonds, which are tied so tight.
Together stand tall, together we fight.
This family bond, as thick as one's blood,
Can even be called to cover a flood.

There's a pride instilled from the day we start.
A fire-fighter's life, blessed with a big heart.
The sense of pride as we travel in red.
That blue flashing light, the fear and the dread.

Arrive on the scene our training kicks in.
Moving in unison, pride — we begin.
A fireman's contract is the fire won't win.
Brigade fire-fighters, we have a strong chin.

fire's been extinguished, the fire's been put out.
Today a good day, has been a good shout.
All is quiet, work now done, no loss of life.
Regroup be ready... a surgical knife.

We know there will be a tomorrow, another day.
We know people are safer with the role we play.
We know that there is pride in everything we do.
We know many people are thankful for this crew.

81

Despair

What's it drives us to the depths of despair,
 Blackness of heart, where we no longer care.
 Got to be... most dangerous of places,
 Clearly see, recognise — many faces.
We move through life attempting to survive.
There comes a point, we're no longer alive.
Move with rhythm, a life the world to see.
Looking really close, you'll find it's not me.
This race try hard standards set by a yard.
Little conviction we've drawn a bad card.
Deep into despair now sink, no return.
It is an endless sleep that we now yearn.
Mind set to auto, the mode day by day.
Lightness to dark confused, think I would say.
Most who know not what they want or they feel.
In this timescale, can now see that it's real.
Think, can we accept, condition our mind.
Darkest of moods, some an illness would find.
Triggers sending down to these depths are wide.
Most when we get there, lock the door and hide.
Advise now, seek help, to turn this around.
For most common people, not to be found.
When we most need support, left in our hands.
Medical profession, won't share their plans.
Often must stand here alone in the dark.
Our thoughts lead from this life to disembark.
Those lucky have proud family, and friends.
Power of love, pulls us back in the end.
Signal, shed a tear deep down from your soul.
Strong surface, yet you're as weak as a foal.
Those who read people, step up to the plate.
Help us to get through this, truly a mate.

Chapter Seven

Comedy Poems

Sadness, grief, pain, anger, despair, loneliness, stress. Now depressed, crushed. Just some of the negative emotions we can experience, counterbalanced by laughter using those complex muscles in your face to share a smile, and receive one in return, is a lift as great as any.

This section is written in the hope it will raise that SMILE, frown and you frown alone, SMILE and the world smiles with you.

Smile!

If you can find a way to smile,
that sweetest look that's held awhile;

Endearing, sure, you will become,
sought by so many for your fun.

Spreading sunshine, just show your teeth;
rarely, folk take a look beneath...

If in this world, you want many friends,
Facial expression - friendship sends.

Outside our space, to take control,
a simple smile will steal their soul.

When life is measured - here and gone,
a smiling face we can count on...

Like magnets pull, warmth will attract;
life in your favour, you'll have stacked.

Happiness, something we all seek...
just for a day, even a week.

With so much misery out there...
come, loving people, show you care.

Be that bright person all beguile;
wake-up each morning - with a smile!

Widgets And Grommets

As we patter the stairs, climb up to our beds,
put a dent in the pillow to rest our heads.
Warily, widgets and grommets are already there,
they are hiding from view, on wings in the air.
There are good ones and bad ones, ones in between;
there are light ones and dark ones, ones that are mean.
Pull the duvet tight, as you wrap it around;
like a comfort blanket, it's warmth safe and sound
Your twisting and turning you kick and you thrash,
that seal that you've made, they're commencing to trash.
Scarily widgets and grommets now get in;
affecting your mood, the next day to begin.
There is little control in who gets there first;
using teeth and their claws, start quenching their thirst.
They climb into your brain, possessing your mind;
awake to the light, they are nowhere to find.
Now controlling your mood, either light or dark,
seemingly every day, they can leave their mark.
Just what can we do to avert this attack,
perhaps not go to bed, do not turn your back!
These widgets and grommets they hide, they await,
yes to affect your mood, to affect your fate.
Maybe, a shot of brandy under the bed,
the bad ones to drink perhaps mess with their head.
The goodies, I'm confident, they do not drink,
ensuring future moods, are good ones I think.

NOTHING BOX

Women's brains are said to be a ball of wire wool,
memories are etched upon them, randomly you fool.
Welded fixed with strength, for the glue is emotion,
flit from place to place, confusing conversation.
A man you see is organised, box files they use.
Each subject marked, stored away, never to confuse.
Unfortunate... access is one file at a time,
as man copes with single subjects, surely no crime.
The box files labelled clearly, we are organised,
However, just one box, most women will despise.
It's labelled our NOTHING box, a place we can go.
If most ladies had their way, in the bin would throw.
Times we're asked the question, "what is it you're thinking?"
Reply bemuses — NOTHING, said without blinking.
They don't understand, impossible to comprehend,
drifts to his NOTHING box, when in need of a friend.
For us a sanctuary, a box we would not fore-go,
little piece of heaven, man has his quid pro quo.

Christmas Past

'Tis Christmas time, it would seem, which now has lost it's edge.
Distant memories — flying deer with a flying sledge.
A red-suited ball of a man with a long white beard.
Many kids sat on his knee with some they even feared.

Things as children we would do to fill our sacks with toys.
Even saw some little girls run up and kiss the boys.
Now as the years roll by, it's meaning is not so strong.
Watching our grandkids fight, it is for our beds we long.

We've surely missed the essence of what it's all about.
"Our lord the saviour was born," is what I hear you shout!
For some this has some meaning, but never has an end.
Yet many it would appear, he's there to be a friend.

Now Christmas new arrives there's no stopping it I hear.
It's not grown-ups that chant, but the children who all cheer.
Perhaps a little unfairly — we who've had our day.
Should sit back relax and let the young ones have their say.

As Christmas lights adorn the house, decorate the tree.
Christmas cards for everyone so please, don't forget me!
With age I've become a grouch, just appeal to my youth.
Cut my Christmas dinner up I've only got one tooth.

The presents are all piled high, the children reach a pitch.
That twinkle has just returned, those presents you do switch.
Tearing paper they're opened, boys get girls, girls get boys.
They all sit there in silence figuring out their toys.

You have had your fun it's time just wipe away that smile.
They know what you have done you had better run a mile.
Wait they all seem to have found a great sense of humour.
Identify your female side, is not a rumour.

There you sit, with your new pinny on, and up you jump.
Once the washing up's complete back in your seat to slump.
Now inhale take a deep breath, for things are really fine.
With both heart and eyes open, enjoy this Christmas time.

Internet Dating

I've read your profile and seen your face.
My opinion you're still in the race.
Button's been pressed the search now online.
We're all scouring, for someone who'll shine.

Modern equipment desktop and all.
Just there to help us, make that first call.
Hurdles seem high, door shuts in our face.
Tenacity keeps us — in the race.

Chemistry seems a well used desire.
If drugs needed a chemist I'd hire.
All that I need — just some willing arms.
Surround me and cuddle, work their charms.

I know it's loneliness we all hate.
The prescription for which find a mate.
Love, to cherish look after for life.
Subliminal challenge find a wife.

Searching... interests, matching our own
Opposites attract, once seeds are sown.
There's no answer it's not rocket science.
Face-to-face meet has that reliance.

Come on meet the challenge of today.
"YES" to that coffee meet me I pray.
All I muster my smile and my charm.
End of our date we'll walk arm in arm.

All has been said my pen has gone quiet.
Hope in my heart our date is a riot.
Meet, talk, in each others eyes we look.
Future mirrored could be the first hook.

Sunday Roast

What is the meal that I like the most.
It's sitting down to a Sunday Roast.
No matter if playing guest or host.
The meal that's best is my Sunday Roast.

Anticipate those crispy baked spuds.
Gravy poured over the plate it floods.
The choice of meats, from chicken to lamb.
Eyes bigger than belly, plate you cram.

There are bits that add that Midas touch.
Cauliflower cheese, like very much.
Fruit and veg we're told eat five a day.
With this meal, on ONE plate I would say.

Beware now your plate's not piled too high.
Knife and fork rested, you take that sigh.
One notch — the belt you try to relax.
Vision elastic waistband on your slacks.

Moving cautiously to an arm chair.
Lower yourself, your mind not a care.
Your next adventure sleep is the quest.
Your Sunday Roast for now to digest.

Chapter Eight

Family and Friends Poems

I would think a lot of people who write, draw inspiration from family and friends. I know I have both been asked to write poems for specific events, and also written poems when moved to do so.

This chapter includes a number of these works, which I hope you will enjoy.

All Three

Today his arms surround all three,
God's children to become
in his house, there's a welcome mat,
for all, not just for some.

Bethany Catherine, the eldest,
young woman we all see;
Her future days, yet still to grow,
her Godmother – Debbie.

Molly Sarah, she's a little star,
her future, is the stage;
With Lauren's hands, to help support,
just watch her come of age.

Ella Hope, her name chosen for all,
with mischief in her eyes;
Sarah, who is now watching on,
will see her win first prize!

Zoe and David who will oversee
our three beautiful girls;
Watching them through to womanhood,
maturing ~ into pearls.

This congregation we all know
our girls will help support;
Along the road, should danger strike,
its power will help thwart.

Supreme love is from Mum and Dad;
live a happy life — never sad.

Eyes of a Child

Delight through the eyes of a child
clasping his father's hand;
wonderment, a family day out ...
imagination grand.

So many places his mind leaps;
electrifying heart pounds.
Deafened, as blood rushes through veins,
picking up body sounds.

Riding the underground north bound;
destination unclear.
Wimbledon Common both alight;
signs so large, "CIRCUS HERE!"

Walking upon soft, dewy grass
towards the smells and sounds.
An unreal world, this queue doth lead,
all smiling with the clowns.

Entering Big Top, worlds away,
everywhere ... magic!
Nostrils filled ~ intoxicating;
Sunny, clown who's tragic.

Seated, almost touch the animals,
as they circle the ring.
Lions and tigers "I love them best";
no, perhaps it's everything!"

In awe, we watch the trapeze swing;
she leaps and she is caught.
Intake of breath from audience;
ending, to our feet brought.

Ninety minutes the purest fun,
a treat for Dad and I.
Together, father and his son;
banked – stored as years go by.

Memories drifting carelessly ...
those times we had were gold.
Wistfully pondering, "which meant most?"
find those you wish to hold.

Misty eyes, tears touch cheeks again;
He breathes ~ his last campaign.

Star Dust

An invite arrived in the post, would you please join us in a toast.
Sam and Paul joining hands in life, she's ready to become his wife.
He, her first choice as a mate, surely nothing here left up to fate.
They've planned meticulous detail, for guests' enjoyment could not fail.
Leez Priory in the back and beyond, memories for all that are fond.
This a day to be there a must, sprinkled copiously with "star dust".
From the day's beginning to its end, we all could find a new friend.
Her day we had to beguile, never seen such a beautiful smile.
Her joy infectious for all to see, one thing in life that's now free.
Take a sip of this nectar true, for one day our troubles all flew.
To have a share in this event, one could believe was heaven sent.
Life has many ups and its downs, we are blessed today with no frowns.
Takes such a day, to commit a lifetime of memories they say.
The hearts and minds of the guests there, together showing that they care.
Giving strength to this union in life, when a husband takes a wife.
Catch a glance in a mirror and see, future years for you and he.
There's nothing unique it's not force, never think consider divorce.
Grow old in love holding hands, walking together on golden sands.
When we all learn to talk with our eyes, whisper goodbye to any lies.
White ones can be alright, it's the black ones seem to cause us to fight.
Share all in this world that is good, live life fully you know you should.
My final hope love now twinkles, still there past all of the wrinkles.
Seeing the future be strong, be bold, touch hands safe in those you hold.
All that is left my pen's laid to rest, this day YES! One of the best.
Something we'll discover, needing two days to fully recover.

Thank You ALL

94

Beth

I have a grand daughter sweet and wise,
She shares her love, there is no disguise.
Her birthday it is here, once "agen",
This year, she has reached the age of ten.

My memories — in my arms so small,
From that first sight and touch, I did fall
Each New Year her mark on me she leaves,
When with her — my heart is on my sleeve.

All children these days growing so fast.
Competing in life, I hope will last.
Setting out ... life's journey to embark,
Growing bigger stronger, make her mark.

What awaits her my feeling is good;
For this young lady, yes anything could.
As she reaches up to touch a star.
I know in her life, she will go far.

All those around her, do wish her well.
On this her birthday, would like to tell.
How much we all adore and love her.
Knowing friends family will — concur.

Love from

Granddad Ken

MOLLY

A proud granddad of little Molly.
Her birthdays here we all are jolly.
Two thousand and twelve she will be eight.
An actress I think will be her fate.

She dresses, struts and she looks so cool.
And yet can be stubborn, like a mule.
In her heart she has always been kind.
Now underneath a young lady find.

Another year has passed by, is gone.
Throughout this year our Molly has shone.
Not shy she will oft be heard to sing.
Like all growing girls she likes her bling.

All that I now have left to say.
Molly have a Happy Birthday.

Granddad Ken xxx

Ella Hope

We've five years now to measure;
as Ella Hope, she grows.
The years fast go rolling by.
A child inside, who knows.

A smile that's full of humour,
a mind so full of fun.
she's, my treasured granddaughter;
my little honey bun.

Off to school to wow them all,
she treads a well known path.
She'll be walking door to door,
she sure, will make them laugh.

Her Mum and Dad they love her,
she loves them back as well.
This gorgeous little red head;
just making all hearts swell.

Two fine sisters Ella has,
Beth and Molly Jordan.
Learn from them, as she grows.
She surely knows she can.

Her Granddad teaches language.
Gobble de gook it's called.
She responds without a thought,
it's others that are fooled.

grigly bifday chinky poo

liv of luv

Grindledad pen

Au Revoir Bill

Dearest Bill, now for us is time to say goodbye.
Words seem so insignificant — however I'll try.
Courage clear, true grit sums up every inch your fight.
Extra time it gave, which certainly seemed your right.

Goes unsaid, the close dear friend you have always been.
Putting both lives together, things that we have seen.
We've both watched technology, move at such a pace.
Indeed this progress helped, to keep you in the race.

This job you've done so well, head your family tree.
Passed on to both your boys, for they now have the key.
Their journey, though not written in tablets of stone.
Your wisdom in their lives, in time they both will hone.

Nova now reflecting — a lifetime to digest.
With all the ups and downs, conclusion, "you're the best."
Decisions now to take supported by your boys.
Remember the best remain strong, serene with poise.

A non-religious man, it's hard for me to say.
Deep down it is my hope to meet again some day.
With inner belief strong, and holding all that's true.
Many good friends out there are now awaiting you.

Bill my friend a request, one job to do for me.
Amongst the many out there, please search you will see.
She is a special person that you need to find,
put your arms around her, in life and death to bind.

Seems in life there's one thing, of which we can be sure
At some undefined point, we'll knock upon his door.
For some it will open, and for some remain closed.
This, my friend, I'm certain, your entry's unopposed.

R.I.P

The Flowers that Blossomed

They both began their lives in Hull.
Gwen with some comforts got.
Stuart's former years were quite hard.
First meet — an arrow shot.

They both worked hard, they fell in love.
Together wished to be.
Engaged and married in their teens.
A future all will see.

His livelihood gained from the sea.
First on trawlers, he served.
Wasn't long before the Navy called.
The world he found was curved.

First child is born, Michelle her name.
To Portsmouth they three roam.
A second child, a son is born.
Whilst Pompey is their home.

Next stop Singapore two years, bliss!
Best memories forged deep.
Luxurious this life they live.
A style for all — to keep.

Back home a new phase to begin.
Mum that wool shop, she liked.
Mark recalls his earliest memory.
She knitted his first bike.

Group4 his future back in the UK.
An upgrade, key to their abode.
Is it fate the sign for flowers?
The Chaffins ~ is the road.

Now retired, fifty years have passed.
Sound marriage most would say.
Still more than happy together.
living in Avon Way.

Your life together is a richness found.
Your family now with which to surround.

Seventy Years

Seventy years have flown, elapsed,
since this young lass was born.
Feisty is her nature... protects,
beware should never scorn.

Growing up her passion is sport;
her great love was net-ball.
Spurs her football club doth cherish,
at her game, she beats all.

Met a guy called Brian, scampish youth,
it's all a part of life.
How the story goes – they fall in love;
soon to become his wife.

Children are on the horizon,
a baby girl is born.
Sarah, being the first child's name.
Over which... both can fawn.

The second is now on his way;
you've guessed, it is a son.
Ian a manly name for the Celts;
from birth he's on the run.

Both wed, families of their own
Doreen and Brian adore.
Grand-children running riot;
counting all... they have four.

Sure this young lady has grown wise;
seventy years to measure.
She's brimming full of memories.
Most of which she'll treasure.

None more fondly than of her ~ Mum.
Kindly woman ~ a harp doth strum.

Long John Clive

Although not therefor all to see;
Your leg now missing from the knee.
Inside there is no change — still you.
Another challenge to see through.

There're times, all face their Waterloo.
It's how we handle... me and you.
Together we show strength of heart.
Whilst grieving for this body part.

Challenges part of life's great plan.
Some we can't deal with, some we can.
Many reasons, burdens, some are.
Full of courage — not au revoir.

Times you have gone in fancy dress.
Pirates' Ball now, "Long John" I guess.
Think clearly, live parrot you'll need;
A crutch, a stump... flagon of mead.

Grab the bull tightly by both horns,
The thing not missed, surely the corns.
With technology, comes great strides,
A choice of limbs NHS now provides.

At first we know it will be hard.
New sprung leg, jump that extra yard.
Poking fun when distressed — not kind.
It comes with friendship, love you'll find.

You're surrounded by love that's deep.
Collected in their arms to sweep.
This support from many — abound.
Not long before you stand your ground.

Your personal warmth spreads so wide.
This scene set — unable to hide.
Friends all there to wish health and strength.
Albeit some, it's from arms length.

Free Verse

Non-consistent meter

Patterns and Rhyme

First in English

1380s

Rhyming Couplets

Each couplet a poem

Equal syllables

10 syllables considered
maximum

Ballads

Four-line Stanzas (Quatrains)

Alternating 8/6
syllables

Rhyming pattern

a,b,c,b

2nd and fourth line
rhyme

Unequal
(offset)

Lines formed into quatrains

Often even number of syllables
10/8 10/8 or 8/6 8/6 no set rules

Rhyme-scheme to best fit
the mood of the message.

a,b,a,b or a,b,c,b or a,a,b,b